The Soul's Journey I

Astrology, Reincarnation, and Karma with a Medium and Channel

Tom Jacobs

Foreword by Steven Forrest

Also by Tom Jacobs

Living Myth: Exploring Archetypal Journeys

Seeing Through Spiritual Eyes:
A Memoir of Intuitive Awakening

Saturn Returns: Thinking Astrologically

ISBN 145152899X
EAN-13 9781451528992

Contents

Acknowledgements...6

Foreword By Steven Forrest 7

Introduction 14

Chapter 1: Paradigms 26

  Speaking Astrology 26

  Ages...28

  The Aquarian Archetype 37

  A Note On Transitions...............................40

  The Mayan Calendar and its End 42

  Astrological Paradigms 44

Chapter 2: The Soul's Journey 49

  Why Are You Here? (Or During Life).................50

  Responsibility, Reflection, and Trauma.................52

  After Life/Between Lives 59

  Timelines: A Question of Perspective.....................61

Chapter 3: Conditioning 68

Chapter 4: Notes on Basics, Aspects and Retrogrades 82

  Notes On Little-used Bodies Used Here.................88

  Retrogrades...93

Chapter 5: Maps of Themes 99

  Majoring 103

Prescriptions 115

Using Themes In Chart Analysis 119

Chapter 6: The Method 122

   1. South Node of the Moon 123

   2. South Node Ruler By Sign........................... 133

   3. Pluto 139

      Empowerment... 140

   Putting The Method to Work 144

   4. The North Node...................................... 147

      The North Node Ruler................................. 150

   Your Turn... 151

Chapter 7: Life Issues And Chart Patterns 154

Chapter 8: Celebrity Charts – Karma...................... 208

   Rosanna Arquette 208

   David Bowie.. 211

   Nicolas Cage 215

   Sibel Edmonds.. 219

   Billie Jean King 225

   Marilyn Manson 230

   Oprah Winfrey 234

Chapter 9: Celebrities – Life And Death 238

   Martin Luther King, Jr................................. 241

   Brittany Murphy... 244

Chapter 10: Suicide.. 249

   The Astrology of Suicide 252

Client Chart 12 256

David Foster Wallace 261

About The Author...266

Acknowledgements

For providing astrologers with a grounded model of how to listen compassionately to clients and thereby allowing astrology to become ever more relevant to them, many thanks go to Steven Forrest. I am also deeply appreciative to him for writing the foreword for this book. For proofreading and editing the text, my thanks go to Lara Gardner. Any errors are my own. Thanks also go to Charity Babcock-Jedeikin for creating the cover.

My astrology students have listened to and explored with me many of the ideas here, and I am grateful to them for their openness and encouragement to spell out the method of chart analysis for others. Thanks go to twelve of my students and clients for sharing their birth data and life stories contained here so that others might learn from them about the soul's journey through many lives.

Thanks also go to my guidance team for teaching me how to ask the right questions and for filling in many blanks when it came to understanding the journey of the soul through many lives.

Foreword By Steven Forrest

Where The Light Is Better

There is the old joke about the man seen searching the ground under a streetlight. A stranger asks him what he is looking for. He says, "My car keys." Then, gesturing with his shoulder, he adds, "I lost them down the street there." The stranger says, "So why are you looking for them here then?" The man answers, "The light is better."

The purely psychological analysis of an astrological chart or a human being reminds me of that joke. To me, the real answers are "down the street," in the realm of prior-life dynamics, but "the light is better" with the less slippery elements of verifiable experiences we have early in this lifetime. Yet there are problems reconciling that psychological model with reality. It is, for example, commonplace to observe that two children born into the same family, of the same gender, fourteen months apart, often turn out to be very different human beings. That is more the rule than the exception it would surprise us if they were truly psychological clones of each other.

Family dynamics are important and leave their mark on us all, of course. That is not in dispute. Twentieth century psychology, and the kind of astrology it spawned, is a powerful, helpful tool that has helped pull many a soul back from the brink. But like any compelling hypothesis, we begin running the risk of mistaking it for the truth. Witness nineteenth century pre-Quantum, pre-Relativistic physics, for one example. In that kind of science, we humans thought we were right, but we were almost completely wrong.

Often, when we have succumbed to the sweet seductions of certainty that way, in retrospect we realize the clues to a deeper paradigm were there right before our eyes all along. Often they lie in the "loose ends" of our observations. Those nineteenth century physics experiments worked "most of the time." Ditto for twentieth century psychology. It too works "most of the time."

But what about when it does not work? What clues do those failures offer? To me, they point directly to something that anyone can see with a single glance into the eyes of a newborn infant. Somebody is already home.

How did that person get in there? What is the source of our observable pre-birth development as human beings? A lot of modern people would invoke DNA as an answer, and I have no argument with that view. But throughout the Eastern religions, Druidism, and much of the pre-Christian metaphysics in the West, we find the idea of reincarnation. And not only the idea of it, but strong evidence for it as well. Even Carl Sagan, the arch-Druid of twentieth century science, acknowledged that fact. In his book The Demon Haunted World, he wrote, "At the time of writing there are three claims in the ESP field which, in my opinion, deserve serious study: (1) that by thought alone humans can (barely) affect random number generators in computers, (2) that people under mild sensory deprivation can receive thoughts or images 'projected' at them, and (3) that young children sometimes report the details of a previous life, which upon checking turns out to be accurate and which they could not have known about in any other way than reincarnation."

If we have lived before, and suffered back then the slings and arrows of outrageous fortune, how could we possibly understand the present psyche without contemplating the lingering emotional effects of those experiences? If we, for example, died horribly in Dachau or at Wounded Knee, how could we understand our present fears and attitudes without contemplating the effects of that nightmare? How could we in all seriousness focus instead upon the trauma of potty-training in this present life?

But of course the problem is that, unlike Wounded Knee or Dachau, most of us have fairly direct access to at least some data about our unfortunate potty training experiences. Past life material is more difficult to access. For most of us, those old memories do not survive the process of death and rebirth except in emotional, attitudinal form. This has made the rational study of the effect of unresolved prior life issues difficult. This is why, collectively, astrologers and psychologists have mostly been looking for the car keys under the street light. The light is indeed better.

In my time, I have seen a renaissance in the integration of astrology and metaphysics. Often under the banner of Evolutionary Astrology, a number of us have been slowly learning how to extract out of the natal chart the underlying information about prior lifetimes. We get hints of that process in Dane Rudhyar and the British Theosophical astrologers. We see it blossoming with Stephen Arroyo and Martin Schulman a generation or two ago. Ray Merriman coined the term "Evolutionary Astrology" in the 1970s. Jeffrey Wolf Green and I, independently of each other, began using the term in our own work in the 1980s. Since then, the wave has broken. A new generation of astrologers has arisen, Tom Jacobs among them. They are surfing that breaking wave and carrying these chaotic ideas forward.

I say "chaotic" in a mood of celebration, by the way. Evolutionary Astrology today is the wild west. Ideas are colliding, going fractal, spinning off in new directions. Everyone knows "there's gold in them thar hills." Enough of it has been panned and brought to market that there is no doubt about that question anymore. But there are many different approaches to the subject, many schools and many contradictions among them.

How to resolve them? How do we carry Evolutionary Astrology forward into a more coherent, consistent system? How do we sort the wheat from the chaff? This brings us back to the core issue. The basic checks and balances that come from having reliable data with which to compare our theories are hard to secure. Past lives, while pivotally powerful in shaping our present lives, are difficult to analyze in that the information is so subjective and slippery. We are trying to connect A and B, but B is often hidden inside a black box. We are tempted to go back to looking "where the light is better." But that is foolish. We must instead try to bring some light to bear upon where we actually "lost our car keys." We astrologers must gain other perspectives on the prior life data. To me, this is currently the cutting edge of this branch of astrology and really of the emerging depth psychology of the twenty-first century in general. I am excited to see, for one example, people who work with hypnotic regressions to prior lifetimes correlating their data with Evolutionary Astrology. The work of Patricia Walsh and Roger Woolger stands out in my mind in that regard. Linking information received psychically or intuitively to that which emerges from astrological analysis, especially when done "blind," is fertile territory too.

Tom Jacobs observes human reality acutely, and to me that will always be the heart of the matter astrologically. "A" is astrology and "B" is the present realities people are actually experiencing, inwardly and outwardly. In that process of observation and correlation, honest astrology thrives, whether we are looking for prior life information or more immediate material. And, in any case, underlying those immediate existential realities are all the clues regarding prior-life dynamics, if we can only see them. But to Tom Jacobs' capacities as an acute observer, we can add another avenue of understanding, the gift of communion with the spirit world. Anyone can of course claim that, but you can judge this tree by its fruit, which I think you will find sweet and nourishing in Tom's case. These insights from disembodied beings combined with his own natural insights and his solid training in Evolutionary Astrology places him and this fine book on the cutting edge of not only Evolutionary Astrology, but also the emerging paradigms of sacred psychology.

I thank Tom Jacobs for sharing his gift with us all, and for carrying the torch forward.

Steven Forrest
Borrego Springs, California
March 29, 2010

Introduction

This book discusses the soul and its journey over many lives, outlines how that journey can be read in an astrological birthchart, and then offers a number of example charts with stories from my client files and those of well-known people to bring alive the concepts and their potential to support healing in real, everyday terms. My motivation is to share the background information and techniques so that others can learn to open the soul's story in any and every chart simply, yet also to learn to put what is seen into practical terms to support people in their evolution.

It is a book as much about metaphysics as it is about astrology, chart interpretation, reincarnation, or karma. Astrology as a symbolic language can be used to communicate many different messages, and here you will find it used to convey information about the spiritual journey each person is on, even those who don't or wouldn't if asked identify as spiritual people. As a book about metaphysics, you will find much information that is not often combined with astrology.

If your interest in the book is primarily astrological, give all of the ideas a chance. After reading the whole of the text, you'll find new ways of viewing and understanding a life journey from looking at birth charts.

This material grew as much out of my counseling clients and teaching students as channeling Ascended Masters and working with the spirits of the deceased as a medium. With the Masters, I've had the opportunity to have "classroom time" with a handful of them committed to supporting the unfolding of life on Earth. They have shown me the reasons a soul incarnates in its many lives and how to understand the process of soul-level learning via the kinds of human experience we each have. I have been shown the process a soul goes through when it picks the Earth-bound human lives it will live. I have also been guided back to the end of a previous life of mine to understand what happens at the moment of and in the moments following death. I was shown how that life and its end lead to the next, and how *that* one and its end lead to my current life. These experiences have left me awestruck and even more passionate and committed to assisting others in their journeys in this amazing place, and I'm profoundly grateful for the insights I have received from them. Chapter 1, *Paradigms*, explores the context of what is up on planet Earth that I learned from working with these beings, including the shift from the Piscean Age to the Aquarian Age that we are beginning now.

From discarnate spirits (a.k.a. dead folks still floating around this plane) I have learned specifics about how they perceived their journeys when alive and then how those perceptions shifted once their lives ended and they gained a bird's eye view on themselves. Some of these have been family members of mine, and some have been family members of my clients (sometimes having the chart of the deceased with me when working with them).

Adding what I learned from these beings and spirits to my intellectual and intuitive knowledge of karmic astrology, a unique and wonderful perspective came into focus. When I look at a chart, I look into a person's soul journey. I'm able to see the overarching storyline the soul is engaged in and can explain it to my client in simple terms. I can answer my client's questions about his or her life while guiding him or her to see possible options which can bring him or her into greater alignment with that journey.

Many people seeking help from me find comfort in learn the overarching picture of their soul journeys. Many of us wonder why we are here or why we are alive, and this approach to chart analysis helps answer such existential questions. While the picture painted by this way of looking into a chart is by nature abstract, it can with very little effort be made to reflect the real-life, day-to-day issues that are bringing that person difficulty, and solutions and resolutions they hadn't before imagined can then be discussed.

An Eye On Experience

When approaching a chart, I begin with an analysis of the nodal structure and Pluto (South Node, South Node ruler, Pluto – all by house, sign, and aspect) instead of the Sun, Moon and Ascendant, as we might expect any astrologer to do. I do this because an understanding of the nodal structure and Pluto opens the door to understand a person's soul-level conditioning (how they have been shaped by their experiences), and working with people in counseling scenarios is helped immeasurably by grasping the landscape of their conditioning. This leads me to understand the general parameters of what a person believes and why he or she believes it. Anything I could tell a person in a session will be taken in through the lens of his or her conditioning. Knowing how my clients see the world, and what they think is happening and expect to happen in their lives, opens the door for me to help them understand how to change what in their life isn't working, the reason most people usually go to an astrologer.

Each person is undoubtedly unique, and yet each is shaped by his or her experience. In order to reach them deeply and meaningfully and to assist in healing and gaining insight and clarity (my goal as a counseling astrologer), each person must be met on his or her own terms, or spoken to in his or her own language. This requires understanding the person's background, history, and beliefs, which is to say conditioning. When I speak the language that is astrology with my clients and students in ways that recognizes the realities of how we are shaped by our emotional experiences, astrology becomes more useful than they had ever experienced or imagined it to be. Chapter 3, *Conditioning*, covers this in greater detail.

Notes On Basics, Aspects and Retrogrades, Chapter 4, defines and frames these elements of astrology from the evolutionary perspective, as the method depends in part on how we understand these things. Chapter 5, *Maps Of Themes*, explores the archetypes of astrology in a broad-stroke way that will make clear how each and every facet of life can fit into one of twelve categories. This view on the archetypes is necessary for successful work with the chart analysis method presented later.

Chapter 6 presents the method of chart analysis at the heart of this approach. I learned about most of its elements at meetings of Steven Forrest's Apprenticeship Program. Though it is in a way at the core of what Steven practices and teaches, it has not previously been organized into a simple system. In a sense the method is a great leveler, laying bare the message in any chart to be read simply and clearly. *But instead of dismissing or attempting to smooth over their obvious differences (which is to say that each person is unique), it makes apparent what they **do** have in common so that meaningful, individualized interpretation can follow.*

That meaningful interpretation necessarily includes your human side. Your imagination, intuition, creativity, sensitivity and willingness to listen to a client and respond meaningfully must come into play in a reading that is truly useful to a client. The future of astrology as a healing tool rests in astrologers' willingness to bring their humanness into their work, staying relevant to human clients amid the reams of possible analytical interpretations seen in any birth chart.

The remaining chapters will take you through example charts to see how to put this way of thinking to work. Chapter 7 contains eleven analyses of charts from my client and student files. Each focuses on at least one issue the person presented with and the relevant chart configurations. Chapter 8 looks at the karma and charts of some well-known figures, while Chapters 9 and 10 look at death and suicide, respectively.

How To Use This Book

In this book you'll read about the conditioning of the soul, emotional memories carried over from one life to another, and a method of chart analysis that focuses on the nodes of the Moon and Pluto to see those emotional memories reflected in the chart. Transits, progressions and solar arcs are tools I use in my practice on a regular basis, but the questions clients come in with are answered much more deeply and thoroughly when those tools are applied after the basic messages of the chart are understood. Understanding a client's progressed Venus, for example, needs to begin with understanding what his or her natal Venus is about. If it happens that Venus figures prominently in the person's past life history (related to the nodes of the Moon, its ruler by sign or Pluto), looking at its house, sign and aspects just won't be enough to understand how that person experiences Venusian energy. The soul-journey or karmic approach outlined in this book brings in a component critical to understanding how people live: the emotional memories of the soul's many lives.

The chart method explained here is to teach you to see the fundamentals of a person's soul's journey. It is useful for developing a grounded understanding of where the person is coming from *as a soul*. Once that picture is in focus, transits, progressions, and solar arcs (and other tools) can come into play to help a client's personality come into more alignment with what his or her soul is doing here, while helping the person with the real-world, day-to-day issue he or she came in seeking help with. In other words, use of astrological tools that deal with current events (transits, progressions, and arcs) is deepened and enriched immeasurably by knowing first what the person's soul is here to learn and experience, the present life being one chapter in that soul's multi-life journey.

Traditional approaches to astrology are of course what most people are familiar with. Yet many people go to astrologers looking for something they don't end up receiving. Some look for predictions (and some get them), but most people are looking to astrology as something to help them gain understanding about themselves and add meaning to their lives. Traditional approaches can fall short because, while they can deal with the elements of astrology in some great ways, they do not always deal with *people* in great ways. If the language of astrology is spoken of in mechanical ways (Jupiter transits bring luck, Pluto transits bring destruction, etc.), the realities of how humans are wired and experience life over time are overlooked. We are complex beings with numerous major components to us, and one of my intentions here is to illustrate the importance of taking all sides of us into account when doing astrology.

The Method

The method section of the book is information meant to guide you to learn an interpretive framework. What it tells you is all about a person's karmic history, the feelings left over from his or her experiences in many lives. Once you understand and have mastered that framework, a structure for interpretation, it will be time to take it with you into the realm of dealing with actual, human people in relevant, human ways. Perhaps you will think this goes without saying, but I can't emphasize enough that astrology is an interpretive art built on ideas and sets of data, and not merely ideas and sets of data. We can't know from a chart how a person lives her life, we can only see the energies in relationship to each other in her psyche and field. We have to learn from her how she experiences the symbols in her chart. We have to treat her as more than sets of keywords and data, after all, and how we treat her chart is how we treat her.

You can look at the method as a sort of loose, bare-bones script – a formula. If you have ever read books on how to write scripts, you'll have read that structure is the key to a good one. There are certain essential elements to be included, and in order for them to make the most sense and impact, they need to be presented in a particular order. That's a good way to think of this material: In any person, there's a formulaic way to approach how to understand how they understand the world and their place in it, and by analyzing his or her birth chart in a certain way, you can see what that is.

Many of my clients have been amazed that I know their deepest issues right off the bat, before meeting them. They may assume all kinds of wonderful things about me, but the truth is that by using this structural framework for interpretation I can immediately see the outline, shape, and scope of their soul journeys. The time a person spends with me in sessions can then be used to work on ways to release tension and make changes to their lives, making for an efficient process and providing them with immediate support for their most troubling and persistent issues.

This book in the right hands lends powerful and unparalleled support to deepening self-knowledge and human journeys in general. It sheds light on how we create our life circumstances and why, and it reveals aspects of our deepest selves, offering opportunities to shift and raise our level of consciousness. I offer it in hopes it will shed light on the importance of understanding conditioning and emotional memories from past lives and help more people experience astrology as the wonderful healing tool that it can be.

Consider the following our point of departure.

Definition of Evolutionary Astrology

As developed by Steven Forrest and Jeffrey Wolf Green.

1. An acceptance of the fact that human beings incarnate in a succession of lifetimes.

2. An acceptance of the fact that the birthchart reflects the evolutionary condition of the soul at the moment of incarnation.

3. An acceptance of the fact that the birthchart reflects the evolutionary intentions of the soul for the present life.

4. An acceptance of the fact that the circumstances of the present life, both materially and psychologically, do not arise randomly, but rather reflect the evolutionary intentions and necessities of the soul.

5. An acceptance of the fact that human beings interact creatively and unpredictably with their birthcharts; that all astrological symbols are multi-dimensional and are modulated into material and psychic expression by the consciousness of the individual.

6. An acceptance of the fact that human beings are responsible for the realities they experience, both internally and externally.

7. A respectful intention to accept and support a person seeking astrological help, no matter the

evolutionary state in which such an individual finds himself or herself.

Copyright 2000, Steven Forrest and Jeffrey Wolf Green

Chapter 1: Paradigms

Speaking Astrology

Astrology is an ancient tool, a language of symbols. Its use throughout history and in all cultures reflects the level of consciousness of those using it. We don't always think of it in this way, but it is a symbolic language and can be spoken in different ways and to different ends. Its potential as a language of healing rests in the level of consciousness of the people speaking it, which in turn depends in large measure on the culture they come from, as well as their particular, individual conditioning.

In short, whatever you are looking for astrology to do for you is what you'll find it will do. Whatever your bias, you can speak the language that is astrology in ways that support and promote it. A language is a tool to convey information, and we've all but forgotten that astrology is a language. Many look to astrology (or avoid it) because they perceive it is a belief system or a kind of science. Understanding it as a language of symbols (that is then spoken by individuals interpreting the symbols) goes a long way to open doors to using it in ways that turn out to be very helpful in advancing our understanding of life and our place in it. Using astrology as a symbolic language, instead of keywords, facts and sets of data, is what enables it to be a fantastic tool for healing and growth.

When I began studying astrology and immersed myself in it, I encountered a lot in the astrological literature that patently was (or had an odor akin to) fatalism. It was depressing, and I wondered if I'd have to sit down and figure out my own system or way of doing astrology. But, I'm happy to report, I found the work of Steven Forrest, and then that of Jeffrey Wolf Green. They had already done in concrete terms what I in vague terms had imagined *could be* done to make astrology deeply useful to people in their lives. Their work situating a person's life into the context of a multi-life soul journey was the first thing I found in the literature that clearly and deeply resonated in me, and the ways they each have of speaking the language that astrology is felt right in many ways. The book you are holding represents a next stage in understanding the journey of the soul, building on what they've been up to for a few decades. It in one way puts a finer point on some facets of their work, but it also introduces a bird's eye view of the soul and human journeys gained from channeling and mediumship that is not present in their work.

Ages

You might have heard about the arrival of the Age of Aquarius, that we're now shifting to it from the Age of Pisces. There are folks who like to argue about whether it has begun or not. While that can be in one way exciting, you won't find any of that here. A change of age takes time to complete and there are always people catching wind of the new ways of being prior to it. There are always people dragging their feet and trying not to notice that everyone else has shifted after it is here. A change of age portends a shift in the collective consciousness and modes of organization – changes in how we think of things and ourselves in relationship to each other, the world, and the rest of life. It has to do with energy the Earth as a whole is affected by, and all life on it in various ways adjusts to it. It is a backdrop or climate for the energetic evolution of life on the planet.

As a result, culture and society are changed and grow as they explore ways of being informed by the current astrological age at any given time. Different traditions and thinkers have official dates to offer for its arrival. I counsel people to shift when they feel they are being asked or pushed to shift, when they feel a call inside or outside pressure to do things in new ways and for new reasons. Worrying about numbers and dates won't serve us as we face the energetic changes happening now on the planet. Very Uranian people have long been able to see the ways the Piscean Age doesn't work and as we begin the transition to the Aquarian Age, it is time for a lot more of us to catch up and allow the way things work inside and around us to change.

My feeling is that we're in a "something's in the air" time before the actual shift, which is the beginning.[1] I know many people who have begun to feel the qualities of the shift in their lives now, some of them wondering if it has already begun. If you're feeling a pull to shift into new ways of being (explained below), then you should honor it. The change in Ages is an opportunity for your consciousness to shift, and while you have the choice of whether to go along with it, life can get more interesting and exciting if you do.

From the perspective informed by soul, each and every person alive on the planet is here to encounter this choice in his or her own way. From the perspective of the Ascended Masters I've worked with, it is an exciting time to be on this planet. Being a human on Earth in general is a unique experience in the galactic neighborhood. Here, you can have a

---

[1] I feel it the beginning was in the 1960s, with the Pluto-Uranus conjunct in Virgo and the social unrest and calls for change that accompanied/reflected it. They were traveling together from 1962-1968, yet those living through and born in those years retain the imprints of very Aquarian messages.

physical body through which you feel energy and viscerally experience emotion, and that is unique in all the places that souls can be in to learn what they embody to learn. As we go about our daily lives worrying and complaining about circumstances of our lives and what we have to do and what we don't want to do, this perspective can seem a little out there, but it is true. Being here, we have the opportunity to ground ourselves into the energy of the Earth itself, and therefore have a capacity for creation that is unique. Yet because of the realities of experiencing emotion in the ways that we do, many of us can be kept busy for entire lives just dealing with the content of our emotional experience and not connecting with these ways life on Earth is unique.

The entire cycle of astrological ages lasts roughly 25,800 years. It is called the precession of the equinoxes, and tracks the shifting orientation of the Earth's axis. If Earth were a perfect globe this would not happen, but over time, the Earth's turning on its axis results in this precession. Which constellation the Earth's north axial pole is in is the Astrological Age we're in.

The Age of Pisces
For roughly the last 2,100 years we've been in the Age of Pisces. Pisces is the mode of

   o   adapting to what is happening around us.

- going with the flow.
- taking cues from others; looking around to see what all the normal people are doing, then doing that.
- fitting in because there is a flow we can feel around us and something about it seems to ask us to adapt to it, and it can feel right to do so.
- learning about life by being a part of something greater than ourselves, which can require sacrifice of our individual desires and will, as well as trust of our instinct.

As an example of social reality shaping the last couple thousand years, organized religion and the kind of societies it inspires have thrived during the Piscean Age. People have been willing to do what they are told or shown in order to fit in to the reality that surrounds them, which is ever greater as the majority of us are no longer defined by membership in small groups and tribes. For our kinds of societies to thrive, leadership must be chosen and decisions made for the good of all, or at least the good of the majority. It is therefore an age of masses and hierarchies, in which what is going on at the top is clearly communicated so that the trickle-down effect can happen. Even if we as individuals are very Aquarian and can't wait for things to change, I feel it is important to understand the reasons that the Piscean

Age is good for us, take our lessons from it, and then move on into new Aquarian futures. There is after all an evolutionary reason for each of the twelve Ages, and the big picture of the evolution of life is shaped in important ways by each.

The Age of Pisces teaches us about new levels of cohesion and connectedness to others. We learn about ourselves as members of great societies and movements. We allow ourselves to fit into categories and we learn about ourselves and life through that lens of connectedness, of having things in common with others. If we adapt to the Piscean energy during this time, we learn that there is a larger organism of which we are part, and we learn how to fit our individuality into its fabric as well as how to stand out from it and what it means to do so. This doesn't mean that each of us chooses to fit in, or even that if we do it we will be happy for having done it. It is a strategy for living that during the Age is explored by many in order to further collective and individual evolution.

Doing karmic astrological counseling that includes looking at past lives (and being rather Uranian and so attracting forward-looking clients), I have met and worked with my share of individuals with karmic histories of being shunned, abused, and killed by their communities for speaking and doing things that challenged the cohesion of the group. One subset is that of people having been burned or otherwise horrifically killed after being labeled heretics or witches by the social and religious structures that have come into their own during the Age of Pisces. Their experiences serve their individual soul journeys, and yet there is also a collective experience that everyone in such scenarios, no matter what side of the gallows or bonfire, is playing out. As we try on for size cohesion and connectedness, how much differentiation can we allow? How much is dangerous? What kind is alright to tolerate and what kind not alright?

During the Piscean Age, we at times have been challenged to defend the cohesion of the group at the expense of its constituents, us as individuals. The Pisces way of being says that we all must do what we can to learn to fit in, and when we can't, or don't, sometimes we have to leave the group. Yet the Piscean Age also has to do with connecting directly to the mysteries, the vast unknown truths of existence. Most of the population at any given time isn't prepared to face any truth straight on, and so they listen to what the higher-ups have to say about those great mysteries and truths. Since religion has been entangled in politics for the entirety of the Piscean Age, fear and fearful rhetoric have been part and parcel of our experience with religion over the last few thousand years. The result is that if you perceive yourself in direct touch with the mysteries and the great truths and are not part of the prevailing religious-political order, you may be perceived as dangerous to it and perhaps needless to say, you might not be welcomed and snuggled into its protective bosom.

All of that said, there is nothing objectively wrong with the Age of Pisces. There's nothing bad about recognizing, learning about and adapting to the greater flow around us. There's nothing wrong with doing it if that is what we feel is right for us. Yet it is merely one of the twelve modes of being, and we're on the threshold of a new one, and so we need to allow things to change if they want to.

The Age of Aquarius

The shift to Aquarius from Pisces has individuals pulling out of those mass trends and looking first inward for definition. There are of course people in all ages doing this but during the Piscean Age we get along well together (generally speaking, as we of course still have conflict) when we sense the ways in which we are all connected. From the standpoint of Aquarian Age energy, community is built around shared perspectives and what kind of world individuals want to live in; community is built by choice after enough individuals with vision about the way they want things to go find each other and form one. Aquarius is about individuation, yes, but also about original ways of creating community in terms of who we are as individuals. Aquarius is forward-looking, and when healthy it is always a step ahead of the established structures surrounding it.

Instead of hierarchies and top-down power structures, Aquarian Age life is organized around vision and ideals, egalitarian co-operation and shared ideas. Individually speaking, our capacity for original insight and genius is our Aquarian side, as is the part of us that inherently understands the need to network with others in order to create the kind of world we want to see around us. When that mode informs us as a collective, we are talking about a move to orientating ourselves toward smaller, local communities that offer us a chance to express ourselves fully with others who express themselves if not in similar ways, for similar reasons. The impact on the world around us we can have is then greater, as more people develop and trust their uniqueness and develop something to offer the community.

Table 1: Contrasting Piscean and Aquarian Age Ideals

Piscean Ideal	Aquarian Ideal
Adapting to what is happening around us.	Observing what is around us and adapting if it is good for us, leaving it if it isn't, figuring out our own way and working/living with others with whom we fit.

Going with the flow.	Creating our own way and aligning with others doing the same with whom we fit.
Taking cues from others and looking around to see what all the normal people are doing, then doing that.	Taking cues from our inner vision, then finding others whose visions match or fit with ours.
Fitting in because there is a flow we can feel around us and something about it seems to ask us to adapt to it, and it can feel right to do so.	Allowing our impulse to pursue individuality to take over and saying "no thanks" to group trends that won't get us where we want to go.
Learning about life by being a part of something greater than ourselves, which can require sacrifice of our individual desires and will.	Learning about creating life and culture around us by knowing who we are first. Honoring the impulse to separate from the whole to more personally authentic and free.

These are all ideals, so it is good to keep in mind that people's experiences follow many routes within this framework. Just as during the Piscean Age, many people will refuse to adapt the overarching Aquarian energy we will all live within. Also as in the Piscean

Age, many will choose to adapt and will be unhappy for doing so. Again, each person's journey will determine the kinds of beliefs he or she holds that will in turn determine the choices available to him or her and the resulting experiences.

Much of what is said about the Aquarian Age that I have encountered is, frankly, New-Age fluff. For a few decades there has been a meme circulating in the collective consciousness that seems to imply that when the Aquarian Age arrives, everything will be light and airy and no one will have any problems because people will be free to be themselves and everyone will accept each other. This took shape in the 1960s with the idealistic counter-culture springing up as Pluto and Uranus spent six years traveling close together through the sign of Virgo (1962-1968). It is critical to be realistic about the archetype of Aquarius, to look into it deeply and understand it as a mode of being to understand the possibilities we are on our way to creating.

The Aquarian Archetype

The range of possible expression of Aquarian energy is from utterly and totally free and invigorated to utterly and totally constricted and bored. Each energy working through the lens of Aquarius seeks to choose and create freedom with its expression. Along anyone's Aquarian journey (whether you have a prominent Uranus or a loaded 11th house or Aquarius is immaterial – even those without an emphasis in this archetype have transits of Uranus and through the 11th house to deal with), there are times when we choose and create freedom, and times when we don't. It is the natural way of learning about an energy. More sometimes, less at others; full-bore free today, half-anemically stifled tomorrow.

When we need to break away from established structure (a bottom-line Aquarian invitation), that can mean leaving groups and going our own way. If we are on an Aquarian journey and we don't choose to leave, we will co-create with the universe scenarios in which we are tossed out of the group. When this happens we have to unlearn what we think it means about us. The Uranian process of objectification in order to see things for what they really are, not how we perceive them subjectively, needs to come into play. There is a greater purpose to everything that happens to us (in support of our evolution), and this objective view is needed if we are to move ahead into the new paradigm.

So we go away from the group and do our own thing. The ideal scenario is that we develop that thing, the what we have great vision about or insight into, allowing our forward-looking selves time and space to flesh it out. In the end, we ideally bring it back to others, perhaps even the groups we left in the first place, and offer our vision for the benefit of all. Sometimes what we can envision can't be seen by others (whether they don't notice it or are threatened by it), and we have to let others catch up to our thought process or level of being. Choosing a Uranian path means being at times ahead of the curve and needing to figure out not just how to develop our vision, but also how to share it with others so many or all can benefit. Sometimes that involves a lot of time alone and a time-lapse of more years than we can be comfortable being patient. High ends to Aquarian journeys include egalitarianism and humanitarian pursuits, yet along the way we have to go through a lot of learning about being different and not being understood in order to be driven to take time alone to develop our unique gift.

Another aspect of Aquarian journeys is in allowing others to react negatively to what you are bringing and continuing on your way with detachment. Forward-looking ideas will always challenge the status quo, and those who feel embedded in it will want to maintain their investment in how things work. As stated above, the Piscean ethic about fitting in or else will in time give way to one of allowing new opinions and diversity. We have to be patient as individuals around us faced with change struggle with their resistance to change.

A Note On Transitions

The transition we are all living through is real. It is an energetic backdrop to our existence, the foundation of how we live. Yet if you don't want to change, you don't have to. Some began this shift in the 1960s (when Pluto and Uranus traveled together in Virgo) and can't understand why everyone wasn't then and isn't now doing it. Others will never open to allow their consciousness to shift, preferring the old ways because of the security those ways seem to offer.

If you choose to take the cues floating in the Earth sphere now to change, your life will change as you understand yourself more in terms of your spirituality identity than your physical, historical one. If you choose not to, life for you will continue in the same ways it has. It is all about a choice of paradigms, how one wishes to see and understand things.

The primary opportunities for us during this transition that I have been shown are to know ourselves more fully, and then to trust what we find. Understanding ourselves as spiritual beings means connecting with ourselves as energetic beings, and as energetically creative beings. This requires letting go of the meaning about who we are that we have developed in the course of our histories, both in this life and over many lives. We all have attached meaning to why we have had the experiences we have had (see Chapter 3 for a detailed exploration of this), which is identifying with our histories over our true natures. Much homework for the current transition on the personal level involves altering our relationship with our histories and learning more about ourselves as energetic beings having physical experiences. Trusting what we find in that self-exploration is necessary to get to the next level. Once we have gained this perspective it is hard to turn away from it but also hard to incorporate it into our lives. Mind and ego are no longer the only ones in charge, as heart and intuition now offer much information about how to proceed. Old habits and ideas about life and living come up for review, and if we can trust these new sources of information and the votes they have for how we should choose to live, our lives will change in significant ways.

Some people get to this place via near-death experiences and others via ecstatic religious experience. The transition we are in (getting a whiff of the Aquarian Age being around the corner) offers more people the opportunity to encounter the choice to learn to know and accept themselves as energetic beings, as more than mind and ego, without dramatic outer experiences such as a near miss with death or ecstatic union with the divine. At present there are cues, many of them subtle, that we can ignore or pursue. In our day-to-day living, it comes down to our relationship to fear and how much of it we let into our lives. Again, in the big picture it doesn't matter if you ignore or pursue your cues, as long as you trust yourself to make whatever choice is the right one for you.

The Mayan Calendar and its End

Regardless of what you might have heard about disasters and cataclysms, the Mayan Calendar was devised to track the evolution of consciousness. When it ends in October 2011, the evolution will be complete. Something new will be arrived at, a something no one knows much (or really anything) about. As I have asked my guides and the Masters about what will happen at that time, I've been shown and coached on approaches and techniques for emotional healing to share with people to support their evolution now and leading up to that time. After several rounds of inquiring about the events that will happen then and being answered with a string of tools to help people get inside their histories to change their minds about what those histories mean, I started to piece some things together that were later confirmed by my guides and the Masters.[2]

Carrying emotional debris, what is often called baggage, with us keeps us from knowing ourselves as

---

[2] Sometimes, the best answer they can offer is to withhold one or redirect you (if the question needs to be rephrased or you need to be challenged to figure it out on your own).

energetic beings. How I have often phrased it for clients is that if we are still obsessing or mulling over painful events from the past, we are not able to live in the present moment, which is where and how we can connect with our true natures. **A primary task for continued individual evolution at this time is to alter our relationship with our histories, with our painful experiences and memories, releasing them and ceasing to carry our emotional baggage from the past around with us.** Each time I asked about the end of the Mayan Calendar and was shown tips and tricks for emotional healing, I was being given tools that can help people evolve out of an emotional dependence on who they have been shaped to be by their experiences so they can clear the decks and live in the present tense, learning to know themselves as spiritual and energetic beings, which is learning to connect with who they really are.

This powerful work I have put into practice with my clients and students, and in fact it has changed in important ways my work and how I think of astrology. Emotional healing requires not just talking about the painful experiences and the imprints from them we carry now, not just feeling them, but doing these two things *and then changing our minds about what those experiences and the resultant feelings mean about us.* We need to know ourselves as spiritual and energetic beings, and to trust that version of ourselves more than what we think we are that is based in why we think painful things have happened to us. They have happened to us because we have signed up to experience all sorts of things related to the themes of our soul journeys, not because we are somehow unworthy of love or deserving of pain.

This particular shift in mindset is the first key along the journey of coming to live in the present tense. It is there that we can accomplish what our souls are here to do without creating a lot of extraneous wounding scenarios because we are unconscious of who we truly are, how this human journey works, and what we came here to do. Yet change is frightening, and our willingness to live in terms of our fears and the fears of those around us will determine our experience in the short term.

Astrological Paradigms

The astrology that works for people going forward as we head into the Aquarian Age will not be able to include limited concepts originated, developed, or matured before or during the Piscean Age. A cut-and-dry approach to chart analysis will not only not serve most people but will become glaringly obvious to all those willing to shift as something neither indicative of nor applicable to the ways people actually live. Many are getting wind of that now, hence the success of approaches like evolutionary astrology that look at astrological charts multidimensionally, and admit the existence of soul and that we live many lives. I see this in my practice now, as people who have been studying or practicing astrology for decades get ideas and understanding from sessions with me that bring in the new levels of meaning they have been searching for, showing them their own charts (which is to say lives) in a new light that opens doors not just to further study but to new peace and acceptance of their lives and what they came here to do.

Approaching the symbols of astrology as representative of energy is a next step in astrology. Most people who seek an astrological education or counseling have not been exposed to this idea and it is time for it to be taught on a wider scale. The Piscean way to study and do astrology is to read what others have written and run with it. It is to approach the subject with the mind as being about ideas and facts. The Aquarian approach to astrology (and historically, Uranus/Aquarius rules astrology) involves intellectual learning, but checking in with yourself about what is true for you and what is not (and separating from or going against the mainstream if that is what keeps you free and authentic). The diversity that comes with Aquarius (humanitarianism, egalitarianism, and related –isms lead to diversity) rests on the idea that different truths and varying ways of expressing truth resonate differently with different people, and so learning to trust ourselves as individuals is needed to find those others and make the transition to the new Age.

The Aquarian paradigm opens up space for people to trust their own visions of what is possible. Innovation follows that self-trust, and many new avenues into metaphysics will result from our deepening self-knowledge and self-trust. One area of study I'm excited to participate in and see continuing to develop is understanding health and wellness from the energetic perspective, while beginning to be comfortable seeing the birth chart as telling of routes to healing health issues and maintaining wellness. Our physical bodies conform to what is happening in our other bodies (emotional, mental, spiritual). Looking at astrology in a multidimensional, energy-based way (as a symbolic language) will empower people to work with their health in proactive ways that serve not just to improve the quality of their day-to-day lives, but also help them heal past life issues that manifest as health concerns now. Traditional medical astrology is an essentially mechanistic approach to our bodies, a Newtonian-style perspective that leaves out the emotional body and its experiences over many lives. It is time to catch our medical astrology up to the Quantum Age.

Our emotions are energy and we carry them from life to life. As the details of our various lives differ, the symbols in the astrological birth chart are what reveal the energies we are carrying in our many lives. The emotional energies from other lives will come out as physical issues now and at present, if we consider our bodies from a mechanistic viewpoint, we miss addressing the sources of our issues. Even if we relieve the physical manifestations of particular issues rooted in past-life emotional memories (addressing symptoms), we are still susceptible to manifesting them physically as we have not seen and processed the root feeling or energetic issue. It is like cutting off the stalk of the dandelion and never pulling up the roots. It will continue to grow back until the roots are dealt with appropriately.

As we learn new ways of looking at energies, we learn new routes to expressing them. We can benefit from the karmic healing that can follow learning to make new choices, and these can lead to changes for the better in our health. When we understand the source of an issue, we no longer need to manifest it as a physical health issue to really see what it needs to show us about the energy we are carrying that is out of balance.

However, again, we all have the choice of how to view things. You can choose whatever paradigm works for you, of course! Each of us can choose to step into multidimensional understanding of ourselves, the world and our place in it. My (rather Aquarian Age) suggestion for you is to try on what is available to you, listen with critical ears and an open heart, and trust your judgment about what is true and meaningful and what is not.

Chapter 2: The Soul's Journey

Who Are You?

Well, you are you.

You are your personality, memories and history. You are your preferences, desires, fears and passions. Your body, the people you come from, your relationships.

That was easy, right?

But you are also something more than those things. Something important is *behind* all those things. Contemporary new-age wording goes that "you are spirit having a human experience." I find this handy when I get tripped up over some circumstance or difficulty with the physical world in my day-to-day life: *Yes, this annoying thing is really happening, but there is something more going on behind it.*

I'm not going to debate the concept of soul here. I'm going to proceed as though we are on the same page regarding the existence of an energetic component of us that exists beyond our physical body and particular personality we carry in this life. It is the thing about us that we cannot quantify but also find it hard to deny. It is the thing that is here with us now, but is more than just our personality, or lasts beyond our time on Earth as physical beings.

You can call it many things, but for the purposes of this book let's just agree to call it "soul." This book is predicated on the fact that we have many lives, and that there is some part of us that exists in all of them. I call it soul.

Why Are You Here? (Or During Life)

Why do souls have chapters of human experience? Why do we do this? My understanding from working with the Masters is that each soul is a portion of the great big divine thing that makes up everything. Each is in a way split off from that whole and on its own journey, so that the great big divine whole can learn about itself. This is happening so that it can learn about what it is like to feel separate from the whole by perceiving discrete entities. When the great big divine energy is whole and undifferentiated, there is no way for it to learn about itself. It is just sitting there being itself without opportunities for reflection from other beings, something each being needs to learn about itself.

We split off, come here, bounce off and play with others who are doing the exact same thing. We are learning about what it is like to perceive ourselves as separate from the whole as we gain understanding about possibilities available to us while incarnated in a place like this in bodies like these. Free will is the single most important component of the learning we do here. We can choose to do anything we want with our time, energy, bodies, and attention, and this is a big part of the experience of the Earth game.

Exploring free will (and dealing with the consequences of our choices) is what underlies each soul's journey, in fact. When we talk about the soul's journey over many lives and healing the debris from the past, we are fundamentally talking about healing a history of having made choices and dealing with the effects of those choices on ourselves and others.

Each of us in any given life is creating a life to reflect past-life memories, whether as an echo of it or in spite of or in opposition to it. The memories result from our experiences and were shaped irrevocably by our choices in those lives. Each of our lives is in a way a recreation of other lives our soul is living, as we choose various scenarios in numerous lives to give us the chance to explore the themes we have signed up for at the soul level. We sign up to explore themes and draw experiences to us that fit with the themes in order to learn about them (see Chapter 5 for this explained in detail). Another way to say it is that each soul has an agenda, and its many human lives are explorations of it.

Responsibility, Reflection, and Trauma

Responsibility

We experience over time and over many lives all sides of the themes on our agenda, and we learn from all of our experiences. We have signed up for the themes behind everything that has happened to us.

It is difficult to accept responsibility for everything that happens to us. Of course it is! A good deal of it is painful and we can find it incomprehensible why we would sign up for pain. We like ourselves and enjoy being happy, right? Yet accepting responsibility is absolutely critical to understanding and working with the soul's journey, not to mention healing ourselves at the soul level. If you have picked up this book on any level to help yourself (which is why most of us are drawn to astrology and spiritual work), spend some time trying this on for size:

Remember a time in your life when you were betrayed, shamed, or hurt in some way. See how easy it is to accept that you created that experience to teach you something important at the soul level, even as it hurt. Try on for size that the painful experience taught you something you needed to learn, because all experience teaches us what we came here to learn. Accept the circumstances and the result as perfect.

How does that feel? Getting inside that is beginning the paradigm shift from "things happen to me" to "I create my reality." It is tough, no doubt about it. This book is ultimately to help you make that transition if you choose it.

If you have signed up for a theme that involves for example exploring power through sexuality (a side of the Pluto/Scorpio/8th house theme), in some lives you are going to figure out how to experience a deep level of trust with precisely the right sorts of confidantes and partners, and in other lives you will be afraid to open yourself enough to find those people, or afraid to express yourself if you do find them. You will be guarded and very choosy about the people you invite to play with you. With that theme in some lives you are going to be blissed out from grounded, mature, spiritual tantric sex. In other lives you are going to experience one or more varieties of sexual abuse.

We have to understand what a theme encompasses (see Chapter 5, *Maps of Themes*) and then accept that we have had real-world experiences in our various lives of all sorts of manifestations of them, good and bad...and then really good and really bad. Dealing with someone shaped by karma (emotional memories that get structured into conditioned belief systems) in this theme as an example *does* involve work with the realities of the emotions behind the bliss resulting from deep connection or rage resulting from violation. Yet healing begins when knowing why the person has manifested painful experiences. There is a soul mission; there is a point to all of this, even the trauma.

You sign up for themes, not specific events. Many factors lead to how you manifest those themes: cultural background, economic status, religious attitudes, and others. A unique benefit of approaching astrology from the evolutionary angle presented in this book is that once it is clear what themes you have signed up for, an astrologer can help you choose explorations of those parts of life without having to feel subject to the worst circumstances. You can upgrade your consciousness and choices about an energy and change aspects of your life experience. This results in using an energy proactively, instead of feeling used by it.

Energies associated with the themes for which we have signed up at the soul level are going to come to us in our day-to-day lives. This is a simple fact. None of us can escape space-time realities reflecting our soul's journeys. We can however in many ways choose what that looks like. To those of us with more traditional-minded approaches to astrology, this may sound absurd. Chances are that if you have studied astrology at any time in your life (other than evolutionary astrology), you have encountered the same fatalism that I did when I began my study – *Jupiter transits bring good things, Saturn transits bring other-than-good things.*

The ability to change the quality of our life experience by learning about the journey of the soul and then learning to choose new ways of doing things is an amazing thing. Take the example of intense sexuality. If you know that this is major part of your soul's journey, you can learn to approach your sexuality with the deep sense of honesty, open eyes, and willingness to experience that this theme calls for. You will have an eye on how important it is to choose the right people to trust instead of being focused on whom you can't trust (a common result of the trauma associated with living this theme). It may require healing memories of past experience, *but you have the option to pre-empt a need for life to bring you experiences that might be damaging.* This is applicable to all of our themes. The door is open for people to radically change their lives by gaining new levels of self-awareness and making new choices.

Reflection
When we are not happy with our experiences or are experiencing pain and trauma, we can take what is happening to us as reflective of what is going on inside us. Once we take responsibility for all that has and

does now happen to us, we can see what is coming to us to be experienced as reflective of where we are on our journey and in our learning.

Each of our experiences fleshes out in the real world what is happening inside us. Not just the themes we have signed up for, but our beliefs about parts of life and people related to the themes, which is to say karma. Everything can be traced back to energy, and our life experience is created around us by the energetic patterns we hold within us.

If I'm having conflict with a friend over an issue, there are two things going on. First there is the issue in question and the need we each have to explore what is going on in order to strengthen our relationship, perhaps a boundary issue or a trust issue. Second, each of us has to look at *why* we are having the experience, why we would need to have that particular experience. I have to look at the tenor and theme of the conflict as reflective of something I need to see about myself. If it is a boundary issue, perhaps I need to deal with a pattern of not establishing good boundaries, and maybe I need to have some strife in order to see this. The other person is holding space for me to see this by experiencing the conflict with me.

All the people we draw into our lives are reflective of what is happening inside us. They are all teachers for us as we go about our learning journeys. My friend is showing up to support me in learning about conflict, and I'm showing up for him to do the same thing, or something similar. This extends to our families, where the lessons we show up to help each other learn are major ones, tending to be more numerous and often more important than others that come up for us in our lives. Family provides an incubator for us, a learning lab of ideas and training about how to live on Earth as a human. *This is the kind of work people do, this is what people believe, this is how people eat.* We have each signed up for the families we are born into and those in which we grow up (as well as those we create around ourselves), asking to be taught by others and to have the opportunity to teach them.

The birth order in the family and the particular relationships matter much in this process. In various lives we offer to be the parents, grandparents, kids, and siblings of each other. We trade roles back and forth, exploring different ways of relating to each other. Looking at the reflection of your family relationships, what you are supposed to be seeing about yourself through the lens of your particular family, is an area I find utterly fascinating. Supporting people in uncovering the truths behind their family dynamics can help them radically change their lives for the better, as deep and lasting as the conditioning we experience in our families usually is.

Trauma

Trauma is the result of experiencing injury or stress. Events that affect your physical person and internal fears that lead to stressful states can result in trauma. Not everyone experiencing an event is imprinted in exactly the same way; what would traumatize one person might not traumatize another. Different people, therefore, will have karmic histories of responding to potentially similar traumatic events in different ways.

I like to use the example of severe weather events. Let's take a mudslide, and look at two people who lose their homes in it. One might respond with utter despondency, feeling abandoned by life and left with a desire to give up trying to have safety and security, two things homes can represent. His neighbor might end up with the idea that starting over might be a good thing, that maybe she was too attached to her possessions anyway. Each will have the same literal experience of losing everything (or at least what couldn't be carried out before the mudslide). Each will be faced with finding a new place to live. And yet they are imprinted differently by their experiences.

Trauma can be physical, emotional, mental, or spiritual. Our spiritual selves are directly informed by our other three selves, and so trauma to our physical, emotional, and mental bodies can extend into being spiritual trauma. There are many resources to be had about the signs of trauma and how to heal it. My focus here is to point out that when trauma is present in any part of us, the vocabulary of astrology can be used to see it. Many of us have some sort of trauma in our karmic histories, and if it is an issue now, we need to deal with it, to clear space inside us to do what we came here to do. Regarding life on Earth, though, trauma is par for the course. We all have experienced it, and we all will experience it again. It is the result of many kinds of Earth-bound experiences, and as life on Earth involves learning to deal with living in bodies like these in a place like this, trauma and its healing are necessary parts of all of our journeys.

Where trauma is present, it is probable that routes to healing other than astrology need to be explored once words are assigned. Some issues can be talked through with success, and others simply cannot. Some people can release trauma quickly once the twos and twos of the soul's mission (why he or she would manifest violence to the self to learn something) are put together with either some crying or emoting (or a lot) or meditative practice or a mixture of the two, yet many need other tools and often other practitioners.

After Life/Between Lives

While alive we have an attachment to ego that dissipates when our life ends. When we pass we have the opportunity to see the larger story of our lives, as well as those of the loved ones to whom we were in life most connected. Elements of our personalities remain but the ego-based investment in being right about how and why we lived the ways we did goes away (generally speaking, of course – there are those of us who cling to opinions and biases, and do so for as long as they need to in order to learn what they are trying to learn).

When we pass, if we are open to seeing them, we are greeted by loved ones we trust who have already passed over. They offer an orientation to our new surroundings, and during that orientation the deceased gets a bird's eye view on his or her life and all of her relationships, and how each significant event and relationship fit with and furthered the journey of her soul. I have heard stories from them about what they understood they were trying to do, the inside scoop on the soul-level goals they learned of after passing and often, they are able to reconcile many of their choices as they prepare to reincarnate again for another round of human opportunity and experience.

We hear of spirits "going to the light" and such. In my experience there is a door that opens to this place, and a discarnate spirit can see it if he or she is open to seeing it. On the other side of that door, if the spirit is open to seeing them, are the loved ones waiting with open arms. It often happens that someone dies in despair or having lost hope and is not open to seeing those who are waiting, in which case a wonderful service a medium can provide is what is called spirit rescue and release (counseling that spirit so that he or she can resolve the emotional issues present at death that prevent an openness to moving ahead in the other realms). The eventual result (when the spirit is ready) is to move "into the light" and be greeted by the waiting loved ones. What follows is a debriefing and orientation, offering greater insight and understanding than was possible during life, when a certain limitation on perspective was in place (most of us don't connect with our souls while living and learn the lessons consciously – not yet, anyway).

Timelines: A Question of Perspective

To live on Earth in these kinds of bodies, we live within and according to the rules of time. There is a time before we as physical entities exist. We are born as tiny, adorable, helpless, and squirmy beings. We grow and mature. And then we die. There are chapters of our experience based in when we are born, how we age, and how and when we die. Everything here depends on this relationship with the physical, and being tied to time.

When focusing on the journey of the soul, understanding our time and experiences on Earth takes on a different shape.

From the soul's perspective, time does not exist; there is no such thing as time.

The soul exists outside space and time. As far as the soul is concerned, all of our lives are happening simultaneously. The general, inner emotional landscape we carry with us is being carried in all of our lives and from the soul's vantage point, simultaneously.

In a meditation, I was shown Figure 1 by a Master to help me understand the relationship between the soul and the lives it connects to on the Earth plane, the lives it is living to explore the human-on-Earth thing. Each white box represents a discrete human life, a birth followed by some amount of time and then a death. While each has a beginning and an end, each is associated with the soul (which has no beginning and no end).

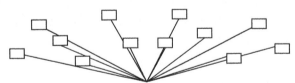

The Soul Is The Source And Has No Beginning Nor End

Figure 1a: The Soul's Relationship To Its Many Lives

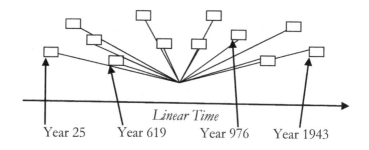

Figure 1b: The Soul's Relationship To Its Many Lives
And Linear Time

Each of the discrete lives can be thought of as
"eruptions" into space-time undertaken to live a life
on Earth. Space-time (in which we live our human
lives) is its own dimension of existence, and the soul
does not belong to it; the soul enters space-time at
numerous junctures to live lives in order to experience
what it is like to be here. Each of these eruptions is a
human life.

Each life serves perfectly the soul's desire to learn
what it is like to live on Earth in human bodies,
subject to the realities of space-time, bouncing off of
other souls having the same experience. Each life is an
extension of the soul, and since it exists outside space-
time, information and experience gained in any life is

accessed by the soul, feeding its mission. All lives associated with any given soul, in other words, provide it with what it came to Earth to experience and learn.

The content of the information fed back to the soul is emotional energy. Our memories are emotional energy, and karma (conditioning and beliefs) is emotional memories strung together to make meaningful stories ("If I do X, I'll get hurt," etc. – the emotional memory is at the root of the conditioned belief). Any given life contains each of the themes that the soul is experiencing over a series of lifetimes, and so what is in a person's birth chart shows the themes of the soul's journey as it is learning in many lives.

It also happens that we shift back and forth between a handful of themes in different lives. We go at themes from different angles in different lives. If the soul is learning about making new choices in relationship, in one life in the birth chart Venus could be conjunct the Sun or Moon (tying relating to the person's identity), in another Libra will house the South Node (indicating a focus on all things about learning Venusian themes of balance, harmony and fairness). In some others, Venus will be square the nodes (an unresolved issue about fairness and how one chooses and has relationships) or conjunct the South Node (the environments of his or her life are saturated with Venusian energy). Always remember that it is the theme that is more important than any particular chart configuration.

An example from my own story is that I have my South Node (SN) in Cancer in the 10th house and Pluto in Libra in the 12th house. In another life associated with my soul's journey (that took place in the first half of the 20th century, and whose chart and biographical information I have), the man had his SN in Virgo in the 12th house and Pluto in Cancer in the 10th house. He had much experience going with the flow (SN in 12th), and needed to learn to experience empowerment in the social or public sphere (Pluto in the 10th). He was primarily an intellectual, and the shape of my life includes learning to let go of intellectualism and be empowered in the spiritual realms (Pluto in the 12th) while having had much experience living in the 10th house previously (SN in the 10th). Threading this together, he needed to heal issues about being in the public sphere (Pluto in the 10th), while I need to heal issues with being in mystical or spiritual realms (Pluto in the 12th). As I have remembered his feelings about his life and consider them with my feelings about my life, I perceive I'm supposed to let go of attachment to status and public success (10th house) and go back to the 12th house to regain a new sense of empowerment from healing or doing whatever from the past wasn't healed or done in the realm of reconnecting with the spiritual sides of life. But of course I prefer that South

Node (we all do, see Chapter 6 for an exploration of this), so a big part of me wants to stay in the 10th house! And a loud part of me often doesn't want to deal with the wounding in the 12th house, as it is messy and frightening. As someone who could write a book like this I can see the need to do it and obviously have done it, yet there are speed bumps in my personality's willingness to do the work the chart evidences I need to do for growth at the soul level.

We don't have a lot of data on people who are aware of their past lives, let alone the charts of people who lived in other times and who were neither famous nor infamous. Most of us spend many lives in obscurity, yet I suspect that with the energetic changes taking place on Earth at present many more young children having access to their past-life memories (including names, birthdays, and home towns) will be listened to, not discarded as wild imagination or nonsense. In conjunction with this, many more parents will be willing to allow this seemingly difficult information into their lives without attempting to edit the children's memories or expressions. I believe that in time there will be much more opportunity to explore this with charts and biographies. In the meantime, what I can offer you is some relation of my own memories and my understanding of this process in my journey as confirmed by the Ascended Masters with whom I work.

The time after a life, or between lives could be imagined as a meeting in which the soul meets with its helpers and evaluates the input from various lives. Since from the soul's perspective there is no time and all of these lives are happening simultaneously, what is actually happening is that the soul is observing and experiencing the input from all of its lives. An image I sometimes get in my mind is of a soul in a room with its helpers and guides with multiple video screens on the walls tracking the results and impacts of choices on the selected themes in various lives. In this image, the soul sits down with its guidance team and the emotional impacts of choices made in the soul's lives are observed and reported.

The soul registers the experiences and the feelings each human person has about them. Remember that each life teaches the soul what it comes here to learn. If you are learning the theme of boundaries, over in this life over here in the timeline you are giving too much of yourself away, in that other one over there you are not giving anything and refusing to listen to what others have to say. In others you are experimenting with how much to open, how much to give, listen, and share. The impacts of all these choices are being tracked by the soul as positively educational.

Chapter 3: Conditioning

Simply put, conditioning is learning to associate a stimulus with a response.

When something happens that hurts us or fills us with joy, we link the events and circumstances leading up to it and assume there is a link:

> *The teacher gets mad at me when I whisper to other kids during class.*
>
> *When I tell my family's secrets in public, I get in trouble at home.*
>
> *When I forget to put change in the meter, I get a ticket.*
>
> *When I surprise her with her favorite dinner or a weekend away, she is happy.*
>
> *When I hit this little bar four times, I get a pellet.*

And so on.

This is true of things that harm us as well as those that bring us pleasure, but also of things that *seem to offer the potential* to harm us or bring us pleasure. If an event registers in us any sort of high emotional impact, there is the probability that we will string the elements together in a timeline and decide that it is cause and effect. Each analysis of cause and effect along these lines will fit into either a survival or pain-avoidance strategy or a pleasure-seeking, gratification strategy. And while it is often unconscious, going forward we will be attuned to what is happening around us in a manner that seems to offer potential for such situations to arise.

We will attempt to recreate scenarios from the past that brought us pleasure and avoid those that brought us pain. We spend an incredible amount of energy on each of these pursuits! Some people tend toward one more than the other. As a counseling astrologer, clients present with each kind of complaint. Too much pleasure and too much fear are at the bottom of most of my clients' reasons for coming in for a session, in fact. We can also cover one with the other, getting confused about why we're really doing something. Seeking pleasure as a route to believing we can avoid pain is very common, as is investing in our fears so we can't see what makes up happy and gives us pleasure. Being happy creates the risk that it can all be taken away (because at some other time when we were happy, what made us happy was taken away).

The bottom line is that we are shaped by our experiences and that to understand a person we need to understand his or her experiences and the ways he or she has been shaped by them. All of our experiences matter. The families we grow up in, our schools, communities, religious organizations we have been a part of. Any group to which we belong or find ourselves in counts.

Family

What you learned was acceptable in your family when you were young is, we can safely wager, informing a lot of your life today. Whether you embraced what you were taught, or refused it and rebelled against it, you were influenced in important ways by that environment. If you are an adult, chances are you don't live with your family any longer, free to make choices for yourself. But the ways you were shaped then formed parts of who you are, were *formative*, and your continuation or continued rejection of them have a lot to do with who you understand yourself to be.

Whatever was going on in your family of origin (whether birth family or adopted family – the family or families in which you grew up), however you were conditioned, fits with and supports your karmic journey. Your soul picked the family you grew up in to recreate the themes of your experiences from other lives again, so you can have what we could call a starting place, a way to be trained as a human to live in society. All the ways you were shaped by being a member of your family are important to you in terms of how you were shaped by your past-life experiences – there is an echo.

Culture & Society

We are also all trained in what it means to be successful members of the larger societies of which we are a part. Our families function as a conduit and filter of the messages of the larger society it is a part of, yet we are also shaped just by being exposed to a culture. Schools, and by extension governments, have a powerful hand in shaping our beliefs about ourselves and life in general. We absorb the messages of what it means to be good members of the cultures of which we are a part, both local and on a broad scale. A part of us internalizes these messages. No matter how rebellious we may be in reaction to them, they still shape us in fundamental ways.

Other Lives

On one level we are all reliving our past lives. We relive the themes we lived in other lives because we are not finished learning about them. It takes many opportunities in the form of life experience to learn all sides of our themes, which is after all why we come here. When we live literal or near-literal repeats of past lives (being a teacher or doctor or criminal again and again), we are not finished getting out of those ways of living what we need to learn from them to serve our soul journey. Some of us do recreate literal circumstances, and the rest of us repeat the themes we lived with and through in other lives.

Even if we are recreating occupations and other circumstances from our other lives, our present circumstances and choices (and ideas of and sense of self) are not less important. It is simply one way we explore the soul's journey through the landscape of human, earth-bound reality.

It is all about the themes. We might be repeatedly seeking the truth wherever we are. We might choose instead to live through the lens of learning about ourselves through other people, of opening to learn about ourselves and the world through learning to observe and listen to others. Or maybe we are primarily focused on learning what it means to lead others, which involves a lot of decision-making and learning to deal with the consequences of our decisions. All parts of life can be fit into one of the twelve astrological archetypes, and we are all focused on a handful of them as the primary vehicles for our learning about what it is like to be here on Earth doing this human thing (Chapter 5 *Maps Of Themes* explores the themes of life and their correlations to the astrological archetypes).

If you are already aware that you are repeating a lot from your other lives, you might wonder when you can stop. You might be wondering when you get to end cycles of repeating a lot of nonsense! Essentially you get to move beyond a theme when you change your mind about what happens in your life related to that theme, and also the meaning about why you are experiencing it. Let's say you are on your way to learning about ambition, for example. Over time, you will have attached a lot of meaning to what expressing or not expressing ambition means. It is simply a vehicle for your soul's learning, but you will invest a lot of meaning in and about its pursuit. Additionally, you will have developed strong opinions about your history of expressing and not expressing ambition. All of this meaning will be rooted in emotional memories that carry over from life to life, which is to say that they are karma. You get to be done with a theme when you give up generating new karma about that theme or reinforcing your old karma related to it. It is your attachment to the results that leads you to perpetuate old karma.

Along the way, you'll have many wonderful experiences expressing ambition as well as many horrible ones. You'll be imprinted by all of them, and what you choose to believe about why each kind of thing happened to you forms karma. In your various lives you are spending a lot of energy confronting your beliefs, looking at the meaning you have attached to your experiences and either reinforcing or reversing it. Over time, over the course of many lives, if you take the good with the bad and cease to attach meaning to why each happens (the same as accepting that ambition is a vehicle for learning about the human Earth-bound experience), your emotional memories about the results that come from expressing and not expressing ambition lose their charge. You lose your investment in them, and it is this lack of investment that allows you to move on to focus on other themes. All of the themes available to us present the opportunity to learn about life in this way, so from the soul's vantage point it makes no difference what particular themes your soul has chosen to focus on. Each and every one offers your soul the chance to do what it comes here to do.

Emotional Impact
The importance of the emotional impact of our experiences cannot be emphasized enough. What we hold from the past greatly influences how we live today. If we do not take our histories into account, astrology simply cannot address the fullness of who we are as human beings. Understanding how we are shaped by our past life experience was a missing link in the evolution of astrology, from a tool to understand the change of seasons and our place in the natural order of things to one that supports us in understanding ourselves as spiritual beings having

74

physical experiences. Now we can grasp it. Now we are ready. When we take emotional imprinting from the past (including our other lives) into account, astrology is a tool for self-understanding that will take us into the Aquarian Age and into our next stage of evolution.

What we carry from our other lives into this one are our emotional memories from our experiences in our lives. We do not (usually) remember the circumstances of our other lives (our names, the towns we lived in, what we ate, what we wore, etc.). We usually remember the *feelings* we had about them and the world around us. From life to life, our emotional memories are what form the basis of recreating the scenarios of the past so we can explore them again now, so we (hopefully) learn to understand those ways of living and (ideally) learn to make new choices that support our ongoing growth.

When we hold emotional memories, we hold energy patterns within us. They are the content of the vibrations we give off. We then draw to us people, scenarios, and circumstances that reflect those patterns, or match them. Our outer realities then, are generated and shaped by the energetic and emotional patterns we carry within us. This is the law of attraction at work. It works at the level of thought creating reality, and adds in the view that looking at our soul's other lives and how they shape our present lives makes astrology a tool for even deeper healing and even more potent transformation.

This is all about energy. Grasping this and applying it to all parts of our lives is how we can begin the transition to the Aquarian Age.

Conditioning & Karma

Evolutionary astrology begins with the recognition that we incarnate in a series of lifetimes. Conditioning of the present life reflects or, perhaps more accurately, *repeats* the conditioning of past lives. We are living in order to understand what it is to be alive, what it is to have an experience of being human. We live in search of understanding how to live the various themes available to souls having a human experience on earth. In the course of this, we create various scenarios in life to explore these themes, and we live these themes out in our search for understanding.

What happens to us in our day-to-day lives affects and shapes our beliefs, and our beliefs underline and perpetuate our circumstances. *Karma is the collection of emotional memories and expectations and beliefs that we carry from our various lives and in which we remain invested.* We have all lived through wonderful and horrible things in various lives. Our karma has to do with the imprints those experiences have had on us, both good and bad.

Karma is about balance, not justice. Given the systems set up in our societies to address wrongs people make against other people, it might be easy to assume that karma follows the same sets of principles: You do something wrong and then you have to pay for it. Yet the laws of karma operate on levels beyond those of the human mind (what creates our systems of social justice).

Karma is the energy we hold, create and expend; the energy we invest in. Our energetic bodies are what reincarnate. They travel with the soul and incarnate with us in all our lives. Our emotional memories are what guide us to create our lives the way we do, and evolutionary astrology looks at the sum of and details of our emotional memories from those other lives. All the circumstances of our lives can be traced back to the impact of our emotional memories. Our thoughts, and even the structure of our bodies, are affected by our emotional selves.[3]

If we think karma is about retribution and reward (paralleling human systems of social justice), we might expect that karma is fixed. We might believe that what is happening to us is not possibly changeable, that we have to deal with life as it comes (the notion

---

[3] As energy is the bottom line of everything, our physical bodies will conform to what is happening in our energetic bodies. The work of medical intuitives Carolyn Myss, Louise Hay, and others is based in this truth.

that we are just paying back a debt we incurred long ago and so must suffer everything happening to us, etc.). However, looking at karma as the sum of our emotional memories and the beliefs that arise from and are associated with them, karma most certainly *can* be changed. This is important: *If an energy is manifesting as unhappy circumstances in your life, you can heal the painful emotional memories and the beliefs associated with them that are creating the difficult scenario in your day-to-day life. You can change your mind about what it means that something happened to you and thereby eliminate the need to continue recreating painful circumstances that reflect your belief about it.* Astrology in this way is a highly valuable tool of self-transformation, a purpose I think many begin learning astrology in order to to find, and one that is necessary as those who choose it can now come quickly out of the limiting ways of being that have taken hold during the Piscean Age.

There are different sorts of karma, which you can find spelled out in traditional sources. Family, genetic, and relationship karma are among them. Also, in some traditions you will read that some are changeable and some are not. From my perspective all karma is based in belief, and belief can be altered, so karma can be altered as well.

When thinking about genetic and family karma, which might seem overwhelming to consider (being an individual who has to deal with the karma of a large group of people), our part in the system can make a great difference in the karma. We each have the choice about how to respond to the beliefs behind the karma, and our choice leads us either to perpetuate it or break it. The strength of family karma depends upon the members of the family system to perpetuate the belief. If for example a person from a family with racist tendencies chooses not to believe in those ideas and lives in other ways, the family karma is affected.

Moving Ahead

As we move into the transition stage between the Piscean and Aquarian Ages, we all have to look at the people we come from with open eyes and honesty. We have all inherited beliefs from our families about life and the way the world works, about how to make our way in society and many other things. Understanding that we have a choice about relating to the world through the lens of our families, and then making choices we feel good about because they are what we truly believe in our innermost depths, is part of the unplugging from the group mind that is the transition out of the Piscean Age. It is natural to feel loyal to the people we come from, and the challenge now as we enter this transition of Ages is to understand loyalty and attachment, belongingness and security, from a spiritual rather than an earth-bound perspective. The spiritual version of loyalty asks you to be willing to support each other in your growth and evolution, and there are many times when not doing what our loved ones want is actually a good thing for all involved.

This brings up the question of the place of family and heritage as we experience this transition. One of the normal human things to do is to define the self in terms of the people and places we come from. Leaving them can be a source of difficulty. Remember that the Piscean ethos tells us that we will thrive if we adapt to what is happening around us. In the Piscean Age way of being, cohesion and fitting in with your surroundings is what is valued and valuable. In the Aquarian Age way of looking at things, whom one knows one's self to be may outweigh the lineage that person is born into. The bigger picture from the Aquarian standpoint is that we are well served by connecting to people we feel in tune with, people who want the same kind of world as we do. Family structure during the Aquarian Age will shift dramatically, and we will choose our families as often as we honor those to whom we are born. And you thought the nuclear family was in trouble *now*?

As we begin this shift of Ages, many are called from within to separate from their families and the places they come from. The beginning of this transition is the most difficult, as individuals are confronted with the challenge to learn to define themselves in new ways. What we cannot see before we do this is that connecting with our families and where we come from becomes easier once we do so. If we answer those invitations to step a little out of the Piscean Age ways of living, we can establish healthier ways of living. Such ways begin with knowing deeply that we cannot continue in any unhealthy relationship and family patterns we have inherited and have been living with. The more honest we are with ourselves, the clearer we can be with our loved ones about who we are, what we're willing to participate in, and what we are not. This kind of clarity takes a great deal of strength. If you define or redefine family relationships in terms of deep personal truths you find within, these relationships will change substantially. You'll find that some of your people are unwilling to let you change. You will find others who do not even want to talk about any such thing. Still others will be inspired by your clarity, those who want to explore what redefinition might look like. Again, this is the beginning of the shift of Ages. Those of us who go down this road are doing something pretty new. If you are undertaking this, have patience with yourself and with everyone else, especially with those who turn out to be invested in not letting you change.

Whatever happens in this process for us, it is for the best. It will support our evolution in this time of change.

Chapter 4: Notes on Basics, Aspects and Retrogrades

While this is not the place for a full introduction to astrology's basics, it is important to include certain perspectives on basics, including aspects (the mathematical relationships between planets in the chart). The analytical method in Chapter 6 depends heavily on how one chooses to interpret aspects. The following should be considered foundational preparation for the method that follows.

I approach planets, signs and houses in the way Steven Forrest teaches them. What follows is an extremely reductionist version[4]:

Planets are functions of us, the parts – the *whats*.
Signs are methods and motivations of how planets operate – the *hows* and *whys*.
Houses are the arenas of life in which these functions play themselves out – the *wheres*.

---

[4] See Forrest's <u>The Inner Sky</u> [pub info] for a complete treatment of all of these basics.

Planets are parts of us, and *work through the lenses* of signs. The houses indicate *the arenas of action in a person's life where that takes place.*

Aspects: Good and Bad

From the viewpoint of evolutionary astrology, no aspect is good or bad. Each describes a kind of relationship between two energies. How we choose to respond to energies, how they manifest in our lives (related to what we believe about them), is what makes the experience of them feel good or bad.

Evolutionary astrology looks at aspects as the relationships of energies within us, which create the circumstances of our external lives.

Conjunction, 0 degrees: Fusion and Merging

Two bodies or energies that are conjunct are touching each other, and can't be separated. Joined at the hip, dealing with one of them requires or automatically involves dealing with the other(s) as well. A group of three or more bodies in conjunction is called a stellium, and represents an emphasis in a house or two, or a sign or two. All in the group are working in tandem, even if we are talking about half the chart in one grouping.

Conjunctions can seem to be more powerful than a planet on its own, but it is just that there are two or more functions of us working together in that house or sign. There is more energy being expressed in that house and sign than where there are single planets in houses and signs.

Sextile, 60 degrees: Triggering and Stimulating

Sextiles bring the energy of stimulation, of triggering. The two bodies in sextile stir each other to action, and whether this is experienced as pleasant or not is another matter. Think of the energies of a good tickling and a poke in the ribs, and then consider that each can be welcome or not welcome. Sextiles have the energy of setting things off, and how we experience this depends on many factors including how willing we are to be set off by anything, what the two bodies in question are, where we might feel pushed to go from the triggering, and others.

Square, 90 degrees: Friction and Pressure

A square is the energy of friction. Two bodies in this relationship have very different ways of doing things, and they can compete for the final say. Think of tectonic plates on the surface of the Earth pushing against each other from different angles. In time, one of them has to give. Squares therefore bring opportunity for change, as with this friction and tension, eventually something has to give and our circumstances will naturally become different.

Growth from squares can be downright amazing if we are willing to let these issues play themselves out and learn what we can along the way; if we are willing to be changed by them.

Trine, 120 degrees: Boosting and Support
The energy of a trine is supportive and boosting. Whatever two bodies in trine are up to, they seem to speak the same language and have goals that overlap or at least are similar. You have probably heard that trines are good, but it can go either way. If two bodies in trine are underexpressed or lazy, they will support each other in staying that way. The same would apply if they are overactive and portend burnout in a person. There is therefore a stability that can result from the relationship between the two, and we have to ask ourselves what they are up to, and become willing to change things if we are being extreme about action or inaction with them.

Quincunx/Inconjunct, 150 degrees: Misunderstanding and Discomfort
There is a discomfort between two bodies with this aspect. The two energies have nothing in common (neither element or modality), and it is like two people not being sure how to be in the same room together. Inside us we are not sure which energy should win in this argument, and our experience of

the two can range from a regular and charged back-and-forth or consistently letting one win, they are not sure how to exist within the tension they have with each other. If we go back and forth between them, we can learn to recognize that each has something valuable to offer (to reduce the stress of the argument). If we always let one win, we could use some acceptance of the tension in order to benefit from the input of each of the two parts of us involved.

Opposition, 180 degrees: Confrontation and Challenge
The opposition is a standoff between two energies. Each has different ways of doing the same thing, and their opinions are in direct conflict with each other. This can be experienced as a kind of totalitarianism in which one energy puts and keeps the other down, which isn't very much fun at all! It can also be that the two parts recognize the value in being able to see each other in ways each cannot see itself. Between people who can see each other in ways each cannot see the self, a level of trust is required to benefit from the information an opposition offers. Within us we have to recognize the value in each perspective and allow each to exist, making neither right or wrong, taking each kind of information into account when making decisions.

Summary

The potential you interpret with any aspect depends on how you look at things. Below are a few examples of some generic traditional ways of thinking about a few aspects contrasted with generic evolutionary ways of thinking about them.

Saturn Square Venus

Traditional thinking: Difficulty in relationships, trouble with money.

Evolutionary thinking: Realism needs to influence and guide approach to relationships and money.

Jupiter Trine Sun

Traditional thinking: Lucky, happy, successful.

Evolutionary thinking: Optimism and faith can buoy the person up, while pessimism and a lack of faith can drag the person down.

Mars Conjunct Ascendant

Traditional thinking: Boisterous, self-interested, needs to dominate others/be in charge.

Evolutionary thinking: Expression of will and desire paramount for good overall health.

Notes On Little-used Bodies Used Here

In various of the chart examples, I discuss a body or point not in popular use, or one that is but with a unique spin. These are brief introductions to four such bodies and one point that will make appearances in the analyses below. They are not meant to explain everything worth knowing about them, but will provide a context for understanding once you begin reading the chart analyses.

True Black Moon Lilith (osculating apogee)
I use this Lilith to understand a person's relationship with the wild, with nature, and with him- or herself as an extension of nature.[5] The nature of healthy Lilith is to say "no thanks" to being controlled, to live freely by being uncompromising about who we are. People live Lilith stories as they learn about the nature of compromise: *How much about me in the realm of*

---

[5] The mean Black Moon Lilith, the asteroid Lilith (1181) and the Dark Moon are also in use. I haven't found the mean position or the Dark Moon useful, yet I do see value in working with the asteroid. I see it representing an awareness of Lilith issues on a social scale, with an investment in the experience and emotional memories of the suppression of the wild feminine that's less personal and direct than the True Black Moon. I see it active in activists, social workers, and various sorts of advocates for women's rights issues.

relationship is negotiable? How willing am I to remain true to myself and my true nature, no matter what? General Lilith themes include freedom, self-sufficiency, and sacrifice, while the specific ways people live the stories include the range of free, natural and wild to suppressed and abused or punished in the arenas of creative and sexual expression, relationships, and relationships to nature or understanding ourselves as extensions of nature.

Eros (433)

My shorthand key phrase for Eros is "creative passion." In birth charts, it often comes down to what creatively and sexually inspires us. Eros operates on a level on which our creative spark is not differentiated between creativity and sexuality. It is whatever it is that gets us going and lights us up. It is lower chakra energy, and feeds our sense of aliveness. People with Eros stories can live in search of the creative or sexual experience that will bring a sense of magic into their lives, or have that sense and thrive on it.

Lucifer (1930)

This asteroid represents in a birth chart the fact that we all eventually recognize something greater than ourselves, and the choice we make to serve it or not serve it. The Christian approach to this energy is to vilify it. Going back to the Hebrew treatment of the archangel Samael makes the real story (beyond instilling in people a fear of anything varying from the established church/social line as evil) come into focus. Lucifer/Samael issues are existential issues, and therefore central to all human lives. Those living Lucifer/Samael stories explore the right size and use of ego as they navigate the choice to align with something greater than themselves, ranging from deeply humble servants of a cause to egotistical jerks focused solely on self-gratification and self-aggrandizement, and the rest of us as we explore the extremes to try to find the right middle ground.

Arjunsuri (20300)

This archetype is one I have introduced, so don't be surprised if you've never heard of it and can't find much information on it outside my website. It represents the archetypal journey of Arjuna in the *Bhagavad Gita*, the seminal text of Hinduism. Arjuna is faced with doing something with far-reaching consequences, and it doesn't sit well with his conscience. God in the form of Krishna comes to him and instructs him to do what he knows he must do, yet cannot as long as his conscience gives him trouble. People who live Arjunsuri stories are exploring their relationship with conscience, and to whom to go to get answers to their most important questions. This can involve spending a lot of energy not consulting the self when making important decisions, and it can also involve relying only on the self to do so, eliminating the possibility of receiving potentially valuable information from learned and experienced others.

Chiron

I approach Chiron a little differently than most. Two main things to say about how I understand and work with it:

1. I go beyond the standard "wounded healer" ideas about Chiron, to seeing Chiron as a marker of our energetic and emotional sensitivity to others, a heightened awareness of what is going on in their inner worlds. It brings up an invitation to learn to change our minds about the point of pain and suffering. I consider all of our experiences with Chiron's emotional sensitivity to be invitations to answer for ourselves what is the point of pain and suffering.

    What most of us do is internalize the sensitivity we have to the pain and suffering of others and close our hearts. We believe that to shut it out will ensure not having to feel the pain. While channeling information on Chiron and its role in the energetic shifts taking place now on Earth, I was shown that the way through the often burdensome and sometimes life-path derailing

91

Chironic sensitivity is to respond to pain and suffering with compassion. If we close our hearts when confronted with it we persist in and feed wounded states. If we open our hearts, we can transmute the pain and suffering and then use our sensitivity to help others in often profound ways. We can become willing to feel everything we can feel, and then need to learn about how to care for ourselves energetically, a major teaching I feel Chiron invites us to learn.

2. Practically speaking, I see Chiron manifest for people in infancy, with wounded part of them persisting in hurt states and causing us to repeat the wounding again and again in their lives. We recreate the original wounding scenario until we answer for ourselves why we feel pain, and until we can learn to take care of ourselves in the ways we needed when we were very young but didn't receive from our parents. "Inner infant" parts of ourselves need the wounding scenario to be proven true, because the unintentional rejection we experienced from our parents or primary caregivers when infants happened during a stage of our consciousness wherein our parents are everything; are God-Goddess. We cannot reason at that age, and so we interpret their rejection as indicating a valid reason we don't deserve love.

Retrogrades

Lots of people let themselves get a little confused when they find a planet that's retrograde (retro or rx). The thing to know is that the energy of a retrograde works differently than a planet that is direct. Remember that the astrology we are usually talking about is geocentric, with the Earth at the center of all of everything. A retrograde occurs when the orbital cycles of the Earth and another planet make it seem from the Earth's perspective that the other planet is moving backward. It most certainly is not, but it is how things are perceived from the Earth's perspective that matters in astrology.

How it comes out in a person's life is that whatever the planet retrograde, the part of the person it represents will need to find its own way. The person will not be able to follow how other people live that energy, or if he or she does, it just won't work. It will be something less than satisfying, and he or she will feel there is something more waiting to be found out. The way I often think of this is that external models of the energy just won't work for the person. Trial and error is in order, which will probably involve adopting ways of doing the energy that other people seem successful at, realizing they won't work and then, ideally, going one's own way.

One way to look at the evolutionary need behind retrogrades is to consider the possible purposes of an energy being directed inward. Retros are a statement that a person needs to or is ready to cease absorbing other people's ideas of how to live certain parts of life. The reason could be karmic in nature, where in other lives the soul's people are listening too much to the ideas of others (Mercury), believing others' beliefs (Jupiter), or trafficking in the ideas of power as other people live them (Pluto).

All planets and asteroids except the Sun and Moon have retrograde periods. Mercury has three per year, Venus about every year and a half, and Mars one about every two years. Jupiter through Pluto are retrograde about five months each year.

Body	*When Retrograde*
Mercury	Perception, hearing, learning, and communicating work differently. There is a need to learn, think and communicate in one's own way and one's own time.
Venus	Ways of creating fairness, finding balance, choosing friends and lovers, and creating self-worth work differently. The need is to learn to pick people to have in one's life for one's own reasons, and to develop self-worth for one's own reasons.
Mars	Will, assertion, defense, instinct and expression of anger work differently. The need is to act in directions of one's own choosing and for

94

one's own reasons. This could be to recharge after doing too much, or doing too much of others want.

Jupiter   Belief, risk, and faith work differently. There is a need to figure out what is worth believing in, and to learn to take risks for one's own reasons, or to stop taking risks or believing in things for a while to recharge after overdoing them.

Saturn   Discipline, authority. maturity, and morality work differently. The need is to develop these parts of the self on one's own terms and for one's own reasons. It could be to recharge from overwork, or being rigidly moral or authoritarian with unhappy consequences.

Chiron   Energetic and emotional sensitivity and related healing work differently. There is a need to develop energetic and emotional boundaries in new ways, perhaps after absorbing too much from other people, taking on others pain and suffering as one's own.

Uranus   Originality, willingness to be free, and means of creating freedom work differently. There is a need to put a check on individualism, either to do it now for the right reasons (internally generated) or recharge after having overdone it.

Neptune   Surrendering ego and merging with non-ordinary realities works differently. There is a need to find one's own way through surrendering – what to do, how to do it, why and when. It could be to recharge from too much surrender (losing the self), or surrendering to what seemed the wrong thing.

Pluto   The empowerment function works differently. The need is to develop a sense of inner, personal strength for one's own reasons and on one's own terms. It could be to recharge after adopting others' ideas of and routes to power, or butting up against powerful others to the point of feeling powerless.

Ceres   Nurturing, (self-)protection, and (self-)care work differently. There is a need to reconsider what care and nurturing are, who needs what care and why. It could be to recharge from doing too much for others and/or not doing enough for the self.

Pallas Athene The senses of what is right and just, and one's willingness to defend them and protect others work differently. There is a need to re-orient one's sense of what's right and just, and learn to stick up for the self and others for the right reasons – learning what's worth fighting for is needed.

Juno   Commitment works differently. The need is to choose what one is committed to for one's own reasons and on one's own terms. It could be to recharge from being committed to pursuits or people for the wrong reasons, or from experiences with them that left one wishing one had not committed.

Vesta   Dedication and devotion in the spirit of service, and a sense of the religious works differently. There is a need to rethink when and why total devotion and service are needed or worth doing. It could be to recharge after devotion and service to what seems the wrong thing of for the wrong reasons, or having done it too much.

Lucifer   The willingness to align with (and thereby serve) something greater than the self works differently. The need is to define for the self the right size and place of ego. It could be to recharge after too much aligning with what other people think is good, or willingly ignoring what one thinks is good.

Arjunsuri   The path to develop a healthy relationship with conscience works differently than for others. The Arjunsuri need to listen to one's self is turned around in that how a person learns to trust the self might seem convoluted and more difficult than for others.

True Black Moon Lilith   The route to developing a healthy relationship with, and expression of one's wild nature works differently. There is a need to get in deep contact with one's inner world and make peace with the self as an extension of nature.

Chapter 5: Maps of Themes

Speaking the language of astrology from the soul's perspective, the birth chart is a map of a soul's conditioning and conditioned beliefs. It is a map of a soul's experiences, beliefs, expectations, desires, wounding, passions and pains gained over the course of many lives as that soul goes about fulfilling its mission. It is a map of that soul's themes, yet also where it is in its process of learning about them.[6]

A chart indicates the thematic emphases the soul has chosen to experience, those it has not been

---

[6] A key to this soul-based astrology is the understanding that a person's stage of evolution cannot be seen in his or her birth chart. The status of the soul, the state of its evolution, cannot be seen in the astrological symbols. What the birth chart shows us is the relationships of the energies in the person that were hitting the Earth when he or she took the very first breath, which in turn can show us the kind of conditioning he or she has accrued over many lives. A birth chart is a map in space-time with the Earth as the center, and the soul exists outside of its relationship with the Earth.

experiencing, and those that have been explored but need to be revisited. It shows us where the emphasis of action has been, what kind of emotional investment has been made in various themes, and how the soul is learning about life as a human. These themes, available to all of us along on our soul journeys, include self-expression, security, responsibility, equality, surrender, and others.

Astrologically, these themes can be grouped into twelve general categories, reflecting the twelve archetypes of the zodiac. If the major theme in question is the development of security, we look to the archetype of Moon/Cancer/4th house, and vice versa. If Moon/Cancer/4th house are emphasized, we can say with certainty that one of the soul's themes is security. If it is learning about deeper levels of self-worth and value, we look to Venus/Taurus/2nd house. Alternately, if responsibility, service and choice are emphasized, we look to Mercury/Virgo/6th house, and so on. The same goes if we see an emphasis in a few astrological archetypes. We can be sure the person's life is a lot about the themes associated with them.

Table 2: Overview of Themes and Astrological Archetypes

Theme	Planet/Sign/House
Will, assertion, directness, forthrightness, instinct, independence, leadership	Mars/Aries/1st House
Values, resources, skills, self-worth, money, proving the self	Venus/Taurus/2nd House
Curiosity, exploration, gathering, learning, communicating	Mercury/Gemini/3rd House
Safety, security, belonging, connectedness	Moon/Cancer/4th House
Creativity, sexuality, playfulness, spontaneity, being the center of attention	Sun/Leo/5th House
Perfecting something, service, healing, mentoring, exploring being dutiful	Mercury/Virgo/6th House
Relating, learning fairness, harmony, and balance through relationship/partnership	Venus/Libra/7th House
Digging to find the truth, power, attempting to merge, deep honesty, trust, feeling psychological truth	Pluto/Scorpio/8th House
Seeking truth, expansion, intuition, faith, belief	Jupiter/Sagittarius/9th House
Authority, maturity, responsibility, hard work,	Saturn/Capricorn/10th House

morality, ambition, achievement, recognition, respect	
Creating freedom, breaking out of constricting circumstances, originality, genius, working toward a desired future	Uranus/Aquarius/ 11th House
Surrender, going with the flow of greater reality around us, mysticism, altered states of consciousness	Neptune/Pisces/ 12th House

We each explore all of the themes to one degree or another (we each have all the planets, signs and houses in our charts), yet there are a few we "major" in, those in which we are invested in as learning vehicles more than we are the others. While we tend to take a lot of our identity from them, they are simply routes to experiencing being human on Earth.

Each of the twelve themes contains a range of possibility capped by two ends of extremity. With the theme of security, the range of extremes would go from extremely secure to not secure at all, and the same with all the others (e.g., with maturity, extremely mature and not at all mature) all the way around the wheel. While perhaps an obvious point, this proves very important when putting the method of analysis (Chapter 6) into practice and actually working with people shaped by emotional investment in the reasons why things have happened to them. What you see in a birth chart are the emphasized themes and relationships between themes, not where people fall in the ranges of possible expression. If astrology is to be useful to people at the level of soul growth, we need to refrain from assuming where they fall in the ranges and listen to what they have to say about their lives. Letting people tell you (sometimes indirectly) where they are is not only much more efficient than making assumptions, but is a step in the direction of treating them as the complex beings possessing free will that they are.

Majoring

The houses and signs of our nodes and Pluto are arenas of life and ways of being in which we are "majoring". The experiences, intentions and difficulties associated with each theme will depend on our placements, and also the meaning we have attached to experiences we have had surrounding each, as well as our judgments about what we have not yet experienced. Chapter 6, *The Method*, goes into detail about using the themes to analyze charts, but below is a broad-stroke look at how each of the themes can show up if we have a focus there with one of the nodes or Pluto.

The South Node represents what we have experienced a lot of and can do well to grow beyond.

We prefer it because it is comfortable, even if we don't like it. When needing to make quick or important decisions, we will tend to rely on these skills and identities.

The North Node is what we haven't experienced much of and may have prejudices about. We usually don't have these ways of being on our radar, and we need people and circumstances to draw us into learning about it. Growing into our North Nodes means adding this new arena to our comfort zones and habits, not leaving them behind.

Pluto represents the deepest intentions and desires of the soul and its wounding. It's what a person is here to do (whether conscious of it or not), and what that person might be afraid to do. Pluto is on one level about the process of becoming empowered, as we can believe we are separate from everyone else living in bodies like these in a world like this.

For each section below, remember that whether a person enjoys what he or she has experienced is a very different matter than the fact that it has been experienced.

Mars/Aries/1st house

Will, assertion, directness, forthrightness, instinct, independence, leadership

South Node: Accustomed to making decisions, being on the go, defense, rescue, fighting or war, the need to make quick decisions or act on instinct, the need to pack and go at a moment's notice.

North Node: Comfortable with letting others make decisions or need to make decisions with others, negotiation, deliberation, peacemaking, diplomacy. Needs to develop courage, define boundaries and express will.

Pluto: The soul intends to develop and act from self-interest, express will, develop boundaries, develop courage. The wound is from not developing courage or losing it, overdoing courage or will or self-interest, being hurt from not having boundaries, not trusting or acting from one's instinct.

Venus/Taurus/2nd house

Values, resources, skills, self-worth, money, proving the self

South Node: Accustomed to dealing with survival issues, possessions, money, gathering and the use of skills and resources, self-esteem/worth, living how one wishes and according to what one feels is important, stability or the lack of it, normalcy, conservatism.

North Node: Comfortable with intensity, psychological truth, digging below the surface, issues related to power, curiosity about taboos, dealing with death and sexuality, control, interpersonal drama.

Pluto: The soul intends to develop and live according to one's own value system, to develop and live from a deep sense of self-worth, and to gather skills and resources to support those ends. The wound is in feeling unworthy, not being able to respect the self for choices made or what one felt was important.

Mercury/Gemini/3rd house

Curiosity, exploration, gathering, learning, communicating

South Node: Accustomed to issues surrounding learning, communicating, curiosity and exploration, rational mindsets, "prove it to me" or seeing is believing, scientific approaches to life, variety, change, what words and thoughts can accomplish.

North Node: Oriented toward intuition and belief more than reason and science, have a history with risk and expansion, knows without understanding how/why, seeking and feeling truth, thinking big.

Pluto: The soul intends to become empowered as an individual by learning and communicating new things, and by exploring the surrounding world and being changed by what is found. The wound comes from situations in which too many or the wrong questions were asked, having learned things that took away one's curiosity, having learned too much for one's own good, having been punished for speaking, learning, or asking questions.

Moon/Cancer/4th house

Safety, security, belonging, connectedness

South Node: Accustomed to issues of home, family, heritage, nationalism, belongingness and connectedness, who one is in terms of the people and places from which one comes, viewing life through the lens of feeling (which leads to emotional investment).

North Node: Comfortable with issues of work, status, achievement, who one is in terms of what one does, practicality, usefulness, ambition.

Pluto: The soul intends to learn to be empowered by experiencing and expressing emotion, and by understanding the self in terms of the people, traditions and places from which they come. The wound is in too much or not enough emotional expression, overly connected or disconnected from home/family/heritage/nation, losing home or family/connectedness and so feeling untethered/lost/abandoned.

Sun/Leo/5th house

Creativity, sexuality, playfulness, spontaneity, being the center of attention

South Node: Accustomed to issues of leisure, creativity, children or being a child, the present moment, being the center of attention or orbited by others, self expression, art and performance, shining.

North Node: Comfortable with deferring to a group's will, emphasizing goals and the future, objectivity,

Pluto: The soul's intention is to express the self, including creativity, art, having one's opinions and ideas honored and respected, and enjoying life by cultivating spontaneity and playfulness and an openness to pleasure. The wounding is in not expressing the self whether by choice or in being blocked by others, and feeling personally invalidated by the experience. Pain can come from being locked into dreary circumstances where creativity isn't welcomed, or overdoing pleasure-seeking behavior.

Mercury/Virgo/6th house

Perfecting something, service, healing, mentoring, exploring being dutiful

South Node: Accustomed to issues surrounding service, humility, team work or being a part of a larger effort, conscious of inequality or imbalance in roles and relationships, oriented toward detail-oriented work, responsibility, duty, control.

North Node: Prefers and is comfortable going with the flow, could feel powerless against outside forces and not take responsibility or develop a sense of duty, sees little need to be on the go or get a lot done.

Pluto: The intention of the soul is to learn to be empowered by developing skills, attitudes and humility in order to serve others and the world. This involves taking responsibility for making the world around them a better place, one detail at a time. The wound is from taking too much or not enough responsibility, over or under serving others, not achieving what was set out to do (even if it had been impossible), self-criticism for having done nothing, not enough, or the wrong thing.

Venus/Libra/7th house

Relating, learning fairness, harmony, and balance through relationship/partnership

South Node: Accustomed to adapting to realities of existing circumstance, compromise, diplomacy, negotiation, aware of the self in terms of the realities of others, familiar with issues related to justice, fairness, harmony and equality.

North Node: Prefers going it alone, being in action and not waiting for others, individual efforts, decisive action, defense, acting on instinct.

Pluto: The intention of the soul is to learn to be empowered by creating peace, harmony and balance in the world. A primary route to this is learning about the self and life through relationship with other people. The wound is from experiencing violence and tyranny, whether doling it out or receiving it, and unfairness, inequality and a lack of justice. Past experience may have shown them that fairness, harmony, justice and equality are not possible, or carry a heavy price.

Pluto/Scorpio/8th house

Digging to find the truth, power, attempting to merge, deep honesty, trust, feeling psychological truth

South Node: Accustomed to intensity, issues of intimacy and power. Attuned to drama both within and in other people, sensitive to psychological motivations, understanding the self in terms of the feedback of trusted confidants, have been on one side, the other, or both of using and being used.

North Node: Comfortable with not rocking the boat, slowing down, dealing with values and issues of resources, practicality, sticking to the status quo.

Pluto: The soul intends and desires to learn about the true nature of power. This happens by experiencing scenarios all over the spectrum of being powerful to not powerful in many ways, ultimately to discover that true power is in self-knowledge and self-control, not knowledge and the control of others. The wound is in being overpowered, abused, betrayed, having betrayed or abused others, issues about trust, sexual bonding and intimacy in general.

Jupiter/Sagittarius/9th house

Seeking truth, expansion, intuition, faith, belief

South Node: Familiar with issues surrounding belief, religion, philosophy, seeking something outside the self that answers life's big questions, learning about life through new experiences and learning about what's different or far from one's self and environs, familiar with intuition and inner knowing.

North Node: Prefers to know the here and now, interested in what can be experienced with the five senses, exploring the world and gathering data, seeing truth in facts and figures.

Pluto: The soul intends to learn empowerment by seeking truth and exploring avenues in life that seem to or might lead to it, learning to have faith and being inspired about life. The wound is in having believed too strongly in something or the wrong thing, not believed at all, lost hope or faith, become jaded, not getting to seek the truth or being locked into a belief system that didn't offer truth.

Saturn/Capricorn/10th house

Authority, maturity, responsibility, hard work, morality, ambition, achievement, recognition, respect

South Node: Oriented toward issues of accomplishment, status, respect, prioritizing work and public appearances, willing to sacrifice, accepts that life can bring difficult circumstances and is experienced in working through them.

North Node: Prefers being oriented toward inner realities and personal perspectives, wants to do what feels good to do, oriented toward home, family (the places and people one comes from).

Pluto: The soul's intention is to learn to be empowered by developing discipline, competency and authority, and achieving status and respect for that competency and authority. It is also to develop a place for one's self in the world, often through work. The wound is in not getting to work or develop competency and authority, coming to public scandal/shaming, being stripped of authority and power and therefore status. The wound can also be in not maturing to the point of independence, being coddled and not respected as an adult.

Uranus/Aquarius/11th house

Choosing freedom, breaking out of constricting circumstances, originality, genius, networking

South Node: Accustomed to being oriented to future goals, being a member of groups and societies, networking, revolutionary, scientific.

North Node: Prefers issues of the here-and-now, accustomed to being the center of attention or being around those who are, familiar with issues of children, creativity, spontaneity, and pleasure-seeking.

Pluto: The intention of the soul is to learn to be empowered within groups and social contexts, working for future goals or social change. The wound is in feeling overpowered by the will of groups or mobs, not finding the right people to network or ally with, or being sidetracked from one's goals and interacting with allies by some other life circumstance. It can also be in working for the wrong kind of future, as when a person learns of secret values and goals of the cause he or she has worked tirelessly to support.

Neptune/Pisces/12th house

Surrender, going with the flow of greater reality around us, mysticism, altered states of consciousness

South Node: Accustomed to being in situations and circumstances in which giving up control is a major survival strategy, familiar with altered states of consciousness (whether by meditative, chemical or other means, and whether by choice or not), a history of merging and fitting in and being in situations where individuality needs to be sacrificed.

North Node: Prefers to take control, is oriented toward specifics, concerned with responsibility and duty, experienced with humility and/or humiliation, service, teamwork, healing, improving something.

Pluto: The soul's intention is to learn to be empowered by aligning with truths that take one beyond regular day-to-day and egoic realities. This involves surrendering to something unseen and, from the human perspective, unknowable. The wound is in refusing to surrender, surrendering to the wrong thing, feeling overpowered by experiences in altered states, feeling powerless and that there is always something more powerful than the self.

Prescriptions

The themes of our lives are imprinted on us energetically yet how we live them is completely up to us. By default, we experience a theme as we have been taught about it, which will reflect our karma from other lives. Over the course of our lives, we will be challenged to learn new ways to express the energies we're imprinted with, yet much of the time we will rely on our habits. How many times have you relied on your habits and training and felt worse off for it? We each find ourselves in need of learning to do things differently.

Since I began my practice, I have offered clients what I called for want of a better word prescriptions. (Homework has a less helpful connotation, though it is probably more accurate!) If someone came in complaining of something that boiled down to a Mars problem (lack of will, drive, or desire, a history of abuse, unexpressed or extreme anger, etc.), I took cues from the Mars/Aries/1st house archetype in his or her chart to make recommendations for new, pro-active choices and behaviors he or she could adopt to change how things were working. The idea was to change how the person experienced Martian energy by showing him or her new choices for their expression of the energy. The theme of the energy is present in our lives, and if we don't use it we may end up feeling used by it as people and circumstance come in to bring the energy to us. This is true for all the archetypes, not just Mars. We each have all of them in our birth charts and lives.

Using the example of Mars, if a person is having trouble with the planet itself, a prescription could be made that focuses on new ways to use a planet in the 1st house, or a planet or point in Aries. Altering understanding and expression of one affects the archetype within the person as a whole. I worked with a woman who was learning about issues of self-assertion and setting boundaries. She has Mars retrograde in Cancer in the 12th and Saturn in Leo in the 1st house. Saturn's energy can limit the expression and natural functioning of wherever it is, and a retrograde Mars in Cancer in the 12th can have some confusion about how just exactly to do Mars (in Moon's sign in Neptune's house, and retrograde, it can be hard for that Mars to *feel* like Mars). Directly pursuing Mars will involve some trial and error for this woman, yet learning to do new things with her 1st house Saturn will stimulate the Mars archetype in her. By setting healthier boundaries and becoming willing to show more of her creativity and sense of authority, she learned via that Saturn in the 1st about how to "do" her Mars in more healthy ways and for better reasons.

The circumstances of our lives do not change if we do not make new choices. It sounds like the most commonplace, common sense idea imaginable. But when people's lives are constructed around supporting various emotional memories and avoiding others, and they perceive something critical is at stake in that support or avoidance, it can be less than obvious. We tend to be greatly invested in maintaining our lives as they are, until we no longer can for whatever reason. Circumstances can change and force us into making new choices or, equally as prevalent, we get so sick of our old patterns that we cause ourselves to seek new ways to do things.

Whenever something in our lives doesn't work, it can be changed. Change is often difficult, but there are many choices about how we live any energy available to us. Each planetary archetype represents a range of possible expressions and manifestations, and we experience them based on our level of consciousness – what we think the energy is for, and the choices surrounding it we believe we have access to. Changing, upgrading or expanding our level of consciousness leads directly to changing, upgrading or expanding our experience of the energies in our lives.

Changing our experience of an energy can heal excesses, misdirections, and deficiencies in our expression of any energy due to past-life memories of unhappy experiences related to it. Someone with other lives of being berated by authority figures (perhaps majoring in the soul journey of learning about Saturn/Capricorn/10th house – discipline, authority, structure, maturity, morality, etc.) might live with a refusal to learn, embody or exhibit any kind of Saturn energy. The soul mission will involve learning about Saturn energy from other people, and being criticized and berated is one way someone focusing on Saturn can learn about it.

He might now be lazy and never learn to develop or execute projects that require hard work, structure, and discipline. When he learns more about the possibilities of expressing Saturnian energy (instead of expecting that doing Saturn energy of his own volition would result in becoming the kind of person he had such negative experiences with in the past), his emotional memories of unhappy Saturnian expression can be understood in a new light and the karma of his conditioned beliefs can change. It would then be possible for him to allow the karmic memories of negativity to be released, or at least to be re-filed in his consciousness as one kind of expression of the energy among many. Remember that if someone is majoring in a theme, he or she will experience all sides of that energy over time. In the example of Saturn, the soul's journey will involve different lives and many forms and levels of, and probably extremes of, Saturn behaviors and experiences in order to learn all sides of it. We could say that the success of the soul's journey relies on becoming willing to explore new expressions, and this often will not happen until we experience some healing of our memories of negative past experiences with an energy. Making new choices with it changes our relationship to it, and the new experience can be healing. If we for instance have an expectation that Saturn energy is horrible because we have been criticized or abused by Saturn-like people in the past, becoming Saturnian in ways new for us can be freeing. Proving ourselves wrong in such situations can be truly liberating.

When challenged to learn new expressions of an energy, we might think we would have to give up something important about ourselves in order to do it. It often turns out to be true, but more often than not what we have to give up isn't doing us any good anyway. It feeds some part of us wanting to remain in the past, yet living in the past doesn't serve us. If it isn't working, why keep doing it?

Using Themes In Chart Analysis

Looking at the Moon in a birth chart will tell us about that person's feeling nature. How he or she likes to feel, and what kind of things he or she needs to do to create happiness are two provinces of the Moon. Another level of analysis takes into account all the ways the person experiences Moon, which includes the body itself, the sign it rules (Cancer) and the house with which it is associated (the 4th). This approach is based on the idea that energy underlies everything in the chart and our lives.

This kind of looking into a chart gives us layers of information that can help us to understand better the real-life experience of a client with an archetype. There might be difficult things going on in the 4th house as the Moon seems to receive positive energy from a few planets elsewhere in the chart. Or there could be a Jupiter-Venus conjunction in the 4th house (often thought to be good), with a Mars-Saturn conjunction squaring the Moon. Remember nothing in astrology is cut-and-dried, and this way of looking at charts can take you deeper into how a person experiences the energy of the archetypes.

Using a specific placement of Saturn as another example, a person might have a Capricorn Sun in the 10th house, which would look to traditional astrological eyes like success in the workplace or world, with lots of hard work and dedication along the way. Yet if that person has Saturn conjunct, square or opposing Pluto (or Pluto in the 10th or Capricorn), the person carries karmic wounding related to the Saturnian archetype. Developing that Capricorn Sun would in real-life terms (not what an astrologer could assume from working with the chart alone) depend on the person's willingness and ability to heal the karmic debris surrounding the negative experiences in various lives with or as authority figures. With the example of

Saturn opposing Pluto, there would be wounding having come into opposition with Saturnian authority figures or groups. The normalizing machine of society and culture seem in various lives in direct opposition to the soul's deepest intentions and desires. With the kind of painful memories that arise from having your soul's mission blocked by some Saturnian group or person, to inhabit a Capricorn or 10th house Sun will be very difficult until you heal the Plutonian wounding and learn to be empowered in relation to Saturnian influences. Until you figure out that healing, you would not want to become the kind of person who hurt you.[7]

---

[7] See Chart 11 in Chapter 7 for an example of a Capricorn Sun conjunct the Midheaven, a man with difficult karma surrounding the Saturn/Capricorn/10th house archetype.

Chapter 6: The Method

The method of chart analysis is made up of a few simple steps, yet it is not meant to imply that any chart (meaning any person) is simple. Each of us is wondrously and marvelously complex and as a map of a person's soul journey and life, a chart is a map of wondrous and marvelous possibilities.

The method is useful as a doorway to understanding the karmic messages of any chart, which are the core issues of the life that goes with that chart. Regardless of appearances, no chart is any more complicated than another. Each tells the story of an incarnated soul exploring what it is to be a human on earth with other humans. Whether a chart has nine squares involving Pluto and Saturn, two grand trines in fire or lacks sextiles or oppositions, no matter. It is the map of an individual soul's journey in exploring what it is to be incarnated here on earth.

Table 3: The elements of the method in order (each to be considered by house, sign and aspect).

Chart Feature	Significance
1. South Node of the Moon	Environments in which the person finds itself in various lives.
2. South Node ruler by sign	Roles in those environments the person performs in various lives.
3. Pluto	What the soul is in various lives trying to accomplish/learn and what hurts the most in the various lives.
4. North Node of the Moon	What the soul hasn't experienced much of in its various lives.

1. South Node of the Moon

Technically speaking, the nodes of the Moon are the intersections of its ecliptic (its orbital plane around the Earth) with the Earth's ecliptic (the Earth's orbital plane around the Sun). The South Node is where it crosses to the south, the North Node where it crosses heading north.

Figure 2: The Nodes of the Moon

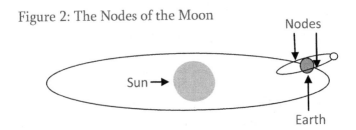

Anyone's South Node (SN) represents environments of the various lives in which the native finds his or her self, the environments the soul is creating around itself in various lives to learn its lessons. This symbolism therefore also represents the person's family of origin in this life and circumstances growing up, and the person's comfort zones and habits. Because he or she has emotional memories of other lives being surrounded by this energy, it represents (usually unconscious) expectations the individual has of what the world is about now. The SN is a major indicator of the social and environmental conditioning the soul is creating to live within, in order to learn what it is here to learn.

Being shaped by emotional memories and related beliefs from our other lives, we will expect the world to reflect what is represented by our South Nodes. We will believe the world to be limited or unlimited, according to the emotional memories we carry. We will believe, and therefore create, a difficult world, an expansive and loving world, a world full of exploration and learning – any kind of world we believe is out there.

These environments reflect the families and communities into which we are born and grow up. We pick our families to provide a context for our soul growth. What this really means is that we choose families to provide a certain kind of environment so we can repeat the scenarios of our many lives, so that we can experience many sides of the themes we came here to learn about and learn to make different choices than we have made in the past.[8]

Again, the themes are what are important. A South Node in the 9th house, for example, will see a person growing up in a family and community group defined by some aspect of belief or the search for truth. It might or might not be religious (including atheism, which is a belief), might or might not be focused on the value of higher education or the importance of law. It might or might not be an international/immigrant or displaced/refugee situation. It might be unhappily pessimistic or enthusiastically optimistic about life. It might or might not be any of the specific things we usually associate with the Jupiter/Sagittarius/9th house

---

[8] The fact that we have karma with groups of people and repeatedly incarnate together as families can add some depth to understanding how this process works over many lives.

archetype, but it *will* be defined by *something* associated with it.

Let's say it is in fact about belief, the South Node here (without considering its sign or aspects) shows us a person who sees the world through the lens of belief. Again, whether belief is considered to be a good thing or not is not the issue. Atheism is just as valuable a vehicle to explore the theme of belief as Islam, Wicca, or Mormonism. The experience of this person in his or her many lives begins with an orientation to belief, and he or she will filter much through this lens.

As everything is about energy, we expect the world to fit the symbolism of our SNs (whether we like that or not is a separate issue), and will therefore find the world to be like it. With a Sagittarius SN, the expectation to finding Jupiterian energy all around will come true because it is held in the person's energy field. If the person is conditioned a great deal by belief, the beliefs of others will be on his or her radar. He or she will be able to pick Jupiterian people out from crowds, perhaps, and may feel comfortable or uncomfortable with such people right away, depending on how he or she feels about the experiences and karma gained over many lives living through this lens.

Aspects to the South Node

Planets and points in aspect to the South Node indicate energies that define and affect the environments of our many lives. The world in which we found and find ourselves was and is shaped by numerous factors, and these will be shown by these aspects. Limitation or tragedy related to war or natural disaster, strategies about navigating life, and cultural attitudes to shape people into certain ways of living are the kinds of things that will show up in these aspects.

Certain energies fill and occupy the environments of our lives. We could be born into a family of musicians or teachers, or a family strongly rooted in particular traditions, whether ethnic, religious, secular, or nationalistic. It could be certain naming conventions, political attitudes, or choice of profession passed down through generations. Perhaps it is an emphasis on creative, scientific, or spiritual endeavors that defines our environments.

Expressions of energies we are taught that are unhealthy or less than proactive show up in aspect to our lunar nodes as unresolved issues. There could be a history of bad relationship choices in our families, or a long line of overachievement and workaholism or underachievement and avoiding work. We could be born into a family of risk takers (half of whom die young or are addicted to gambling), religious zealots who have lost sight of reason, or people who talk a lot but don't talk about their feelings or their true thoughts.

Still other facets of life simply are not available in some times and places. Disastrous weather events or natural disasters could be a part of our real-world experiences in various lives. When you have to scramble to meet basic needs, leisurely creativity and meditation are luxuries. If you live under an oppressive regime, whether fascism in your government or family, speaking your mind or practicing your chosen religion might not be possible if you want to survive. We could also be born into a repressive environments of one kind or another in which personal expression and healthy ego development and gratification aren't acceptable.

The possibilities for each of these kinds of examples are endless. All human experience fits within the symbols and their relationships to each other.

Conjunctions indicate an energy that saturates the environments of the soul's various lives. It is an influence present in large measure. The ever-present or highly noticeable fact of this energy conditions the person's expectations of what the world is like. Over the course of many lives, a soul experiences all sides of the energy, and will therefore be in any given life in many ways experienced with it. Perhaps he or she will not understand how to use it, or how to use it healthily or productively, but various kinds of manifestations of the energy will be familiar to him or her. As it is always present in the environments of the soul's various lives, it can be something that the native takes for granted. For example with Saturn conjunct the South Node, a person may expect the world to be built around hard work, responsibility, or maturity (regardless of how this person lives those energies), or expect to find poverty and hardship everywhere he or she goes. With Jupiter, something about risk and expansion or belief and faith color the environment. With Mercury, learning and communication figure prominently in the environment.

Sextiles are the energy of stimulation. Planets making this aspect to the South Node tell of an energy that functioned in the karmic past to effect or drive some circumstance or outcome of the environment or community. This is an energy that triggers circumstances with the environments, for better or worse. Pluto sextile the South Node indicates that powerful or overpowering people or circumstances affected what life is like in those environments. It could be that uncontrollable forces kept the community on its toes, needing to always be vigilant for a threat. This could be a political or social situation, the threat of an invading army, or potential for a volcanic eruption or mudslide. The reality or fear of the reality of a Plutonian event like these stimulates the environment and has real effects on it.

Squares to the nodes represent friction to the environment and show up in people's lives as unresolved issues. The energy was part of the environments of the karmic past, yet there lacked an understanding of certain aspects or expressions of it. A person with a planet square the nodes may understand some or many appropriate and healthy uses of the energy, but will find that there is something he or she does not understand. This will show up as repeated patterns in which the person is habituated to attempt to solve or resolve in the same way again and again. The solutions employed so far will not feel right, complete, or resolved. *The pattern will persist until he or she learns to make different choices.* One way to think of this is that the person has been conditioned by the attitudes, beliefs, and behaviors of the places he or she comes from; the person has been taught certain ways of doing things. With a square to the nodes, the conditioning or education about the energy has lead him or her to make choices that don't actually work, or don't get the person where he or she wants to go. Learning to make new choices means leaving what we were taught behind, even if it seems to work for us (it is familiar, after all, so we probably tend to prefer it). Venus square the nodes, for instance, means that the values taught by the environment ended up not being enough or appropriate for a person. Values result in our choice of friends, lovers, and mates, and often Venus in this position shows up as relationship choices that are ultimately unhealthy. A person with this aspect will have to see the blind spot about Venus he or she was taught, and learn to expand something about his or her values and then learn to make new choices about who should and should not be included in the ranks of friends, lovers, and mates.

Trines are the energy of boosting, of support. The environments of this soul's many lives are supported by people or institutions representing the energy of the trining planet. Support in this context can mean buoyed up, underwritten, or encouraged. Each of these can be for our benefit or to our denigration, depending on what is going on and how we feel about it. With Saturn trine the South Node, the environments of a soul's karmic journey are supported by people or institutions embodying Saturnian energy. When this is good, the environment is supported by a healthy government or strong leader, or by a solid network of elders. When something other than good, the environment is supported by something more like hardship, limitation, or difficulty. Being born into a family of slaves with strict overseers could fit here, as the strength and hardship of the overseers makes the slavery environment possible and enables it to endure.

Quincunxes represent a fundamental misunderstanding between an energy and the environments of the karmic past. A community or family can be completely knocked off track by a situation or person or group, and this can show up as a quincunx. It is the energy of being not just blindsided, but knocked down and never figuring out how to get up again. It can also be feeling obliterated or knocked off course in total surprise by a person, group or circumstance represented by the quincunxing energy. A person will have a very uncomfortable relationship with people, groups and situations representing this energy, and will need to learn to look them in the eye and deal with them to work through the difficulty they seem to stir in his or her life.

Oppositions to the South Node are conjunctions to the North Node. When a planet or point is in this position, it was as far from the native's karmic past environments as it could be. It is after all fully on the other side of the chart wheel. The energy of the planet or point in question was for any number of reasons not available, including being blocked by individuals or groups in the person's life or by circumstance. Among the range of responses to this lack in the past, a person tends to one of two general responses: Being very determined to have that energy be a part of his or her life (*at last!* – feeling it is deserved or a right), or avoiding it altogether because the native doesn't believe that he or she deserves to have it be a part of his or her life. Some people vacillate between these two extremes, unsure how to put the energy to work in their lives. Not being able to choose one's own marriage partner, for example, might show up as Venus conjunct the North Node. Being blocked from practicing one's religion could show up as Jupiter here, and Saturn could indicate never being expected to grow up and take care of one's self, or being prevented in some way from doing so.

Remember that all of these aspects tell us about where a person is coming from, how he or she has been trained and conditioned to live. The often unconscious expectation that the world is going to be like the South Node and its aspect configuration can make it difficult to get through to someone that change is possible. *It has always been that way after all*, someone may repeat to his or her self, perpetuating whatever circumstance is up for review.

2. South Node Ruler By Sign

This tells us of a person's role in the environments symbolized by his or her South Node. For whatever reasons including talent, willingness or eagerness, being in the right place at the right time (or the wrong place at the wrong time!), the lives of the soul have been shaped by performing a role in his or her family, workplace, community and/or society. It is just one kind of vehicle to learn the lessons of life.

To some degree, a person will expect to inhabit this role now, whether it is an enjoyable one or not. It is what is familiar from the past, and familiarity can trump happiness along the soul's journey. It also happens that others expect us to inhabit this role. Some with whom we have karma will remember our skill, talent or usefulness in that role, others will simply read this energy in our field (usually unconsciously), reflecting our own memories of having performed it.

We re-create this role or function in our environments now usually without any idea why it is happening. It is how in various lives we respond to our environments. When it comes to others expecting this of us, it can be easy to give in to others' visions of us, ideas of how we should behave and live. But, as stated above, they are either remembering us how we were or picking up on how *we* remember we were. We can perform this role again and again and get the same results, whether enjoyable or not; it is on a deep level who we expect ourselves to be and be perceived and therefore has much to do with who we become and how we are perceived.

Aspects to the South Node ruler tell us of the pressures and supports on us in our roles in various lives. They show us with what kinds of people we are inclined to feel comfortable and those with whom we would rather not get involved. The difference between these aspects and those to the South Node is important: *Aspects to the SN ruler indicate pressures on and support for the individual, and this often differs from those to the SN, the environment.*

For example, someone with a 3rd house SN is coming from a context where education and curiosity are highly valued. But if that person has a planet in the 3rd house square the SN ruler (his or her role), he or she receives friction from 3rd house people. The intention is to learn about the squaring energy in this way, but the friction will often be less than pleasant. This could manifest as feeling surrounded by 3rd house communicative or learning energy (3rd house SN), yet pressured by 3rd house kinds of people to change in undesirable ways (square from a body in the 3rd house). Such a person could come from a family in which teaching science and scientific research are highly valued as professions (3rd house). Let's say the South Node ruler is in the 12th house squared by Jupiter in the 3rd. In the family environment this will show up as pressure from the family itself or someone in the family with strong or big opinions (Jupiter) to do things in a 3rd house way instead of a 12th house way, the natural mode of the chart holder's role in various lives. The 12th house is as unscientific as we can get! The natural mode could be more of that of a mystic, so the 3rd house orientation to logic and the scientific method would grate on someone feeling at home in the 12th house.

Sign Rulership

In my practice I tend to use traditional and modern rulers at different times. When looking at someone's chart, I usually know at least a sentence or two about where he or she is coming from, and that helps guide me to choose which to use. There's no hard-and-fast rule for me to offer you; you are going to have to explore this on your own.[9]

Aspects To The South Node Ruler

Conjunctions indicate an energy that is foundational to the role of the individual in various lives. The conjuncting energy is one that is fused with the person's role. He or she will identify as someone carrying the energy of the conjuncting planet. He or she will have developed skills and attitudes related to that energy and carry the energy now, and there will be a strong level of identification with what it means to express it. With Mars conjunct the SN ruler, the person will identify in some way as a warrior, rescuer,

---

[9] You may find that reading the ruler of the South Node as Pluto makes it difficult to then use Pluto as indicating the soul's deepest intentions/desires and wounding. In this case, look at that single symbol as working on two levels.

or leader (or other Mars keyword). Neptune conjunct it would be in someone relating to some archetype of Neptune including mystic, addict, artist, etc.

Sextiles as stimulation indicate an energy that worked to stimulate the native in his or her role in the karmic past. The person will easily form relationships with people representing these energies, and be stimulated or triggered by situations promising or containing it, whether this is experienced as a good thing or not.

Squares tell us of friction to the person in the role he or she was fulfilling. A person will feel tension from anything presenting or representing this energy and perhaps be loathe to develop and inhabit the energy in him- or herself. People and circumstances representing such an energy can comfort the person or be uncomfortable, depending on his or her perception of the energy and how he or she feels about being pressured into change or growth. It is common for a person to experience people and situations squaring his or her South Node ruler as bringing tension. They represent an energy that is trying to make the person change, after all.

Trines are from energies supportive of the individual in his or her role. People or groups that help him or her along fit into this category in various lives. These for example might be the first kind of people to appeal to when help is needed. There is a supportive relationship with this energy in the person.

Quincunxes indicate the fundamental misunderstandings with persons or situations that significantly affected the native's role in the karmic past. Again, encountering the aspect of this energy to the SN ruler leaves one feeling not just blindsided, but irrevocably knocked off course.

Oppositions show us energies that opposed the native in the karmic past. As this is the energy of confrontation, the person will expect people and groups/institutions bringing this energy to challenge him or her, to work counter to his or her aims, and will therefore manifest them in all of his or her lives. The soul's intention is to learn about the energy by being confronted by and with it, yet the real-world experiences we have down that road can be damaging. The details of the opposition (whether a person or group, whether from a parent or not, etc.) will change relative to conditioning and belief in any given life. An example could be Saturn opposing the SN ruler. The person will have had run-ins with Saturnian figures. In a life born into poverty, this opposition could be from government and church groups when seeking aid. In a life born into wealth, a parent who takes care of all of the person's needs could constantly challenge him or her to grow up, confronting him or her with criticism and parent-oriented advice.

3. Pluto

My shorthand for Pluto as the third step in this analytical method centers on these questions: Given what is going on with the South Node (what we perceive surrounds us) and its ruler by sign (what we perceive we are doing here and who we are), what are we trying to do that at times feels like it goes wrong? In what theme or set of experiences are we deeply invested that brings us a lot of pain as we explore it?

Pluto in evolutionary astrology represents two seemingly different things: the deepest desires and intentions of the soul (what we are trying to do), and the deepest wounding of the soul (what hurts the most or the deepest).[10] I combine these two, as I see that when we go for what we most want, we are that much more vulnerable when we do not get it. And since the journey of the soul in human form is about learning about all sides of the energies we sign up to explore, we have all had the painful experiences Pluto can represent in our chart as we go about manifesting in our lives the desire it represents. Yet Pluto is also unconscious, the deep desire in us of which we might not have awareness. We can, however, see it revealed when we look honestly at our behavior and the

---

[10] The idea of the soul's deepest intentions and desires comes from Jeffrey Wolf Green, and that of the deepest wounding of the soul from Steven Forrest. Each has published a very useful book on Pluto.

attitudes and beliefs behind it. What is it we are most intent on doing? What seems the most important thing to get done? What feels like it must be done if we are to feel like we didn't waste our lives? The answers to these questions point to Pluto.

I often think of Pluto as a ball of wonderful, happy, shiny, golden molten goo that is our core power source, our atomic energy source. Surrounding it is a crust gained from experience in the world during many lives. In order to get to the shiny wonderful nature of the golden goo, we have to heal the pain and fear that encases it. Pluto work can be intense, time- and energy-consuming, and is all about facing and processing our deepest fears, and then knowing ourselves in terms of those encounters. Most of us unconsciously engineer our lives to avoid repeating our Pluto wounding and in the process keep ourselves from understanding the root desire behind all those fears, what the soul came here to do.

Empowerment

Each soul in various lives is exploring via Pluto the notion of empowerment. We traffic in external ideas of power until we discover that true empowerment has everything to do with our relationship to ourselves. I suspect that the soul journey each of us is on hinges on our learning how to perceive ourselves separate from divinity/Source/God-Goddess yet remember that we are part of it. Pluto figures into this in that the deepest, unconscious desire it represents for each us can be boiled down to recovering a sense of that connection to the great big thing, feeling empowered as part of the world we live in. Once we do that, once we remember and can tune in to the fact of our divinity (and that this entire soul journey has taught us about all sides of the mission we have undertaken), we can uncover that deepest of desires. I also believe that in each of us the deepest desire is to be of service to the rest of creation, to the rest of us and the world. When all the layers of ego investment are stripped away, when all the veils of our personal investment in the details of our journeys are peeled back, I believe that what we see is a desire to give something to others. Once we recognize our divinity, after all, we can see that of others.

To put it another way, the entire journey of the soul through many lives could be thought of as an exploration of empowerment. We go through a process of realizing that we are in a way separate from the divine thing (whatever you want to call it), followed by figuring out what power is. For most of us it will seem that external power is the apex of it, and we can explore that until we figure out that the feelings available to us from successfully navigating routes to external power aren't really that fulfilling in the end.

Some evolutionary astrologers see Pluto as representing the soul. The soul is not possibly represented by a symbol in the birth chart. Much information about the soul's intentions and journey can be seen in a chart, but the soul itself cannot. A birth chart is a map in space-time of a human life. It is created with Earth as the center, and shows the relationships of the bodies in our solar system. As discussed elsewhere in this book (Chapter 2), the soul exists in a dimension outside the one we live in, which is the one that includes the physical bodies in our solar system. A chart shows how the light of the Sun is reflected off the Moon, planets, and asteroids, and is therefore showing us parameters and possibilities of a human life as it has begun being lived on this planet, in this dimension into which the soul is erupting for discrete periods of experience.

Aspects to Pluto

Since Pluto represents simultaneously the deepest desires/intentions as well as the wounding of the soul, everything about Pluto including aspects needs to be read through this dual lens.

Conjunctions indicate an energy tied up or fused with the deepest desires and wounding of the soul. It is part and parcel of the soul's intentions and desires. Saturn conjunct Pluto says that the soul is majoring in learning about empowerment through discipline, structure, maturity and work. Venus conjunct it is a statement that the soul will learn to be empowered through developing a value system and relating with others.

Sextiles tell us of energies that trigger and stimulate the desires and wounding. People born since the mid 1940s, for example, have Pluto sextile Neptune, representing a desire to use Neptunian triggers to go about empowerment, and the wounding that comes with it from Neptunian sources having triggered us to not get where we desired to go.

Squares point to energies that have simultaneously driven the person to change, relative to the soul's deepest desires, and also energies that have offered friction to the soul. This friction has contributed to the deepest karmic wounding. Energies in this aspect will come up in a person's mind and heart as a reason not to pursue his or deepest desires and intentions, yet once the feeling of friction is turned into learning how make use of the pressure to change, a squaring planet will offer support and pointers for achieving the soul's mission of empowerment.

Trines indicate energies that the person has experienced as supportive and boosting when going after what the soul has most deeply desired. Trines can be experienced as helping to further what we are doing whether we are sitting around doing nothing or highly active and productive.

Quincunxes show us an energy that has derailed us in the karmic past from achieving our goals, resulting in wounding. The evolutionary intention of this aspect is to keep us on our toes so we have to regroup on a regular basis on our path to empowerment, but the emotional imprints from such real-life experiences can traumatize us to the point that we don't pursue empowerment. The feeling with this can be, *If you can be knocked off course so easily after all, why bother doing anything of value?*

Oppositions to Pluto indicate energies that show in up a soul's lives to oppose the desires of the soul, ultimately contributing to its pain and the feeling that what was held most important was not accomplished. The intention is to learn empowerment by being challenged by such an energy. But again, we can feel overpowered by energies in this aspect to Pluto and choose to keep ourselves from becoming empowered.

Putting The Method to Work

I use this method as a skeleton for the analysis of every chart.[11] Because of the multidimensional nature

---

[11] Transits, progressions and solar arc directions need to be considered in terms of the message of the natal chart. The same with relocated and draconic charts. When you begin your analysis by unlocking the message of a chart using this method, the confusion of so many timing elements, etc., is removed. It enables you to focus on the basic idea of the arc

of the symbols, I can't know precisely how any energy manifests in a client's life. Is the unresolved issue of Mercury square the nodes for that person primarily about thinking, listening, learning, or talking? It could be each of these or something in particular, and a chart alone does not indicate which.

The three-step method is some homework for the left brain, to paint a picture of the energetic dynamics of a person's consciousness and life in broad strokes. When a client is sitting in front of me, or if I know a little of his or her biography, I can begin to see realities of how the energies of the chart manifest in his or her life. All kinds of things indicate bits and pieces of how a client might experience the energy, but my norm is to ask them what they want to work on. Their answers (including the content, wording, style, and emotions in the response) tell me how they have been experiencing the energies of their chart, and it is then a simple matter to proceed with getting into the heart of the issue.

For instance, when I see Pluto in Virgo in the 5th house in the chart of a client coming in for a session, I know that the client's soul's bottom line is about learning to be empowered by choosing (Virgo) healthy routes to creative expression (5th house). This could manifest in his life as being terrified to perform

of this person's life, and then add whatever layers of analysis that you wish to, or that seem appropriate.

anything creative (being overwhelmed by Virgo's perfectionist eye), or it could come out in his life as developing expertise in one or more areas of creativity, being analytical and highly skilled in a particular medium or expressive style.

It could instead be that his life revolves around fear of intimacy because of the bogeyman of sexually transmitted diseases, being afraid of a germ-related side of fun and play. When I ask him what he wants to work on, he will make it clear at least one way Pluto in Virgo/5th is present in his life, and we will go from there. However it manifests in his life, studying the symbols from the multidimensional view while staying open to hear from him how he experiences them ensures that I can help him, instead of leaving me go about telling the client how he or she lives.

With these three steps, we can make a story in broad strokes from any possible chart. I make notes in symbolic shorthand for each chart, letting their themes and the relationships between them soak in, often overnight. I allow them possible kinds of real-life stories that people actually live, to bring the themes and those relationships to life. Imagination comes into play, and I remain open to images and metaphors, and archetypes and stereotypes, to let it breathe. Again, I don't know how a client lives her chart until I hear from her about her life, so before working with someone, everything is possible, wide open, and with the potential for "anything goes" within a handful of thematic parameters.

Using the three steps with the chart, so far I've worked only with what the person already knows. Often, doing a reading on just the three steps (or one or two) helps a person put his history into context, which can be very healing. Understanding why life has unfolded the way it has can bring a deep sense of peace. Also, understanding in what ways different choices can be made within existing circumstances is healing and empowering. But there is another piece of the puzzle that comes in after all that history is outlined and explicated, the North Node. Working with the three steps of the chart analysis method is only the beginning for working with a client regarding his or her healing and growth.

4. The North Node

We all have some part of life that gets left out as we go along our journeys, and it is represented by the North Node. It happens that we get accustomed to certain parts of life and become attached to those parts (the SN). In each life we have a North Node to stir us to grow into new territory, and this is really to invite us to bring some energy or experience into our lives to bring balance to our soul journeys. We need to explore all facets of life during our journeys, and we'll always gravitate to some more than others. The North Node tells us what we need to become willing to expand into and add to our repertoire in order to grow.

The North Node is often a blind spot for us. We haven't done a lot of it in our various lives. As it is opposite our comfort zones and habits (SN), we can have ideas about what it would mean to do it. I've noticed we can have prejudices about that way of being, opinions about people who embody the symbolism of our North Nodes. We might have fears about becoming "that kind of person" that the opinions cover up. It isn't just the unknown, but the opposite of our preferences. Who would want to do *that?* Who would want to be *that* kind of person?

Yet there are times in our lives when we're swept, dragged or enticed into that territory, when we're presented with opportunities to explore it. Our willingness to step into the unknown defines these junctures. Will we try something new? Will we take the advice of some trusted other about proceeding from some life juncture with attitudes foreign to us? Going with it takes into new territory and can be very fulfilling, yet it is also often difficult. It is what we haven't done before.

To get to the North Node with my clients and in my own life, I identify the fears and prejudices held about the North Node symbolism and then address them one by one. This gives the rational faculties of a person a chance to weigh in about what is objectively true (none of those opinions!), and opens the door to teaching the person about how he or she can navigate it well. The prejudice we might have represents one expression of an energy, an archetype made into a stereotype and, sometimes, elevated to the status of boogeyman!

For example, someone with a Gemini South Node might have ideas about what Sagittarian energy is all about (forgetting for a moment what else in the chart might be in Sagittarius or the 9th house, or what Jupiter's doing). Gemini values openness and curiosity, and the single-minded focus of Sagittarius can be thought of as not just less than productive, but downright idiotic. *Who would want to be like **that**, closed-minded and unable to learn new things?*, the Gemini SN person might think. *Those people are opinionated, bull-headed, so into their beliefs that you can't reason with them. Myopic, gullible, always pontificating but with no basis for it in reality, always telling you what they know while unable to tell you how they know it.*

Gemini and Sagittarius are simply different ways of obtaining, processing and using information. Gemini works through the lens of openness, Sagittarius through the lens of focus. It is that simple. To have a SN in one of them means to have been trained in and probably therefore to prefer that mode of learning, thinking and communicating, and now with a need to learn to grow in the other direction to provide the soul with more and new kinds of human experience.

It might be tempting to think that each person has a single mission in any life. This is a romantic idea and we might enjoy thinking about what it means to have a mission, a singular thing we are meant to do, but we actually have several missions. Pluto represents the soul's desires and intentions, which is certainly an important mission. We can feel charged with importance with whatever our Pluto is doing or wants to do, even if we don't have words for it when asked. The NN is different in that we need to explore it for growth, but it is usually not something we set out for with intention. In the scope of the soul's education, Pluto could be thought of as what you choose to take a degree in, the NN as the rest of the curriculum you have to take that leaves you well-rounded, having covered more bases than you would have if your deepest desires and intentions were not tempered with something else.

The North Node Ruler

The NN ruler by sign can be used to point the way to the NN, in the same way that the SN ruler showed us more about a person's experience than the SN taken alone. Someone with a Gemini SN, for example, may tend to over-identify with Mercury in its configuration in his or her birth chart, representing his or her role in various lives. Encouraging this person to get to know the North Node ruler Jupiter in his or her chart can open doors into getting to know that energy. If someone has opinions about the NN, addressing the ruler is one way to help the person explore possible ways of using the energy that are beyond those limited beliefs carried over from other lives. Because Jupiter is in fact somewhere in the person's chart, he or she will have at least some measure of experience with it. It is a part of the person, and it can be useful to see how to grow into the Sagittarius NN when Jupiter in his or her life is brought to life and emphasized as a route to soul growth.

Your Turn

Take a few charts you know well, or some from the next chapter of examples from my client files (without reading my analyses yet). Sit down with each and write down keywords for each of the three steps, followed by the North Node. It is fine to use your own chart, but know that your objectivity might be hampered. If you begin with yours, just make sure you also do a few others, too.

1. *House, sign and aspects of the South Node.* What kind of environments is this person used to? What kinds of pressures are on those environments? Are

there unresolved issues there? Are there any energies they are full of? Are there any energies lacking in those environments?

2. *House, sign and aspects of the South Node ruler by sign.* What kind of role does the person have again and again in various lives? How does he or she expect to be treated? What kind of pressure and support will the person expect to find, and therefore will have found? What energies might this person expect to be challenged or blocked by?

3. *House, sign and aspect of Pluto.* What's the soul's bottom line? How is this soul in various lives approaching the process of becoming empowered? What in that process seems to go wrong, perhaps repeatedly? What fears and pain can be healed and overcome in order to get on with empowerment and the soul's mission?

4. *House, sign and aspects of the North Node.* What is unfamiliar to this person? What new territory needs to be explored to round out the soul's education and growth? What prejudices might need to be resolved before growth can occur?

Do this with a few charts, seeing how the method can provide a basic structure to open messages from each and every chart. Each chart viewed this way tells a story, a karmic story. The following chapters are comprised of examples charts from my client files and some well-known people. You can proceed by reading them, or by practicing with the method on some of the charts before reading my analyses.

Chapter 7: Life Issues And Chart Patterns

The charts in this chapter are analyzed in terms of the reason the client gave for coming in for a consultation. This will illustrate how particular elements in the four-step framework can be understood and addressed in ways that help the chart holder deal with issues in his or her day-to-day life.

The analyses here are not exhaustive. Those here do not cover all aspects of the configurations in question, only the ones giving them trouble when they came in for a session. For example, Example Chart 1 has the South Node ruler Mercury in Scorpio/8th house square Jupiter in Aquarius/12th house, yet the difficulty with the inconjunct to retrograde Chiron in Aries/1st house had more to do with what made him come in for a session. The square to Jupiter is important for understanding his karmic journey, yet this way of exploring charts here was chosen to offer a number of examples while ensuring each can be digestible.

The following eleven example charts are snapshots of life issues causing these clients to come in for a consultation, and the corresponding chart configurations with a discussion of how he or she lives the energies and how we worked on his or her karmic situation.

Client Chart 1, Male
November 28 1973, 1:00 PM, San Francisco CA

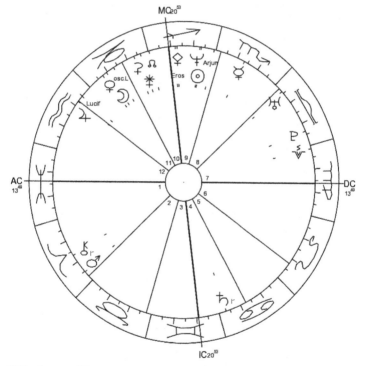

Life Issue: He came to me with a history of what amounted to temper tantrums and was ready to understand what was really going on to move beyond it. He was unsure of how to come out of a lingering immaturity and (at times) hyper-emotionalism, yet knew this was just one part of him and not who he really was.

Relevant Chart Configurations:

1. 4th house South Node conjunct Saturn in Cancer/4th, ruler Mercury in Scorpio/8th house
2. Retrograde Chiron in Aries/1st house inconjunct SN ruler Mercury in Scorpio/8th house
3. Pluto in Libra/7th house square the nodes and Saturn

The South Node is in Gemini in the 4th house, conjunct Saturn in Cancer in the 4th house. The saturation of Saturn-in-Cancer energy on the 4th house South Node speaks of conditioning that has to do with a heavy sense of connection to family, genealogy, and tradition. In his various lives, Saturn energy is very prominent. Along the range of Saturnian expression we find at one end the epitome of maturity and discipline, and at the other end we find laziness, carelessness and immaturity. We can wait for others to do things for us, especially if they are inclined to do so, and delay developing emotional maturity. This man's parents embodied Saturn energy for him. His father is a judge and his mother was an exacting and demanding interior designer. It was easy for him to let other people be mature for him – he was surrounded by it, after all, why should he also have to do it? South Nodes in the 4th house are oriented toward emotionality to begin with (being in the house of the Moon), yet the South Node ruler Mercury in Scorpio/8th, a water sign and a water house, intensifies a predisposition toward living life through an emotional lens.

Chiron in Aries/1st house inconjunct SN ruler Mercury speaks to him having an extremely uncomfortable relationship with issues related to the wounding of will in various lives. This might manifest as being caught off guard and completely derailed by Chironic figures (whether wounded or healer). The resulting emotional imprint is that allowing for that level of sensitivity can only bring trouble. It is a way of being that leaves him hurt in various lives, so of course he would be hesitant to explore it further now. Remember the inconjunct is a totally uncomfortable relationship between two energies. The two bodies are not sure how to be in the same room together. What he is left with now is an assumption that the deep sensitivity he has to the emotional realities of others (Mercury in Scorpio/8th) cannot be directly expressed (inconjunct to Chiron in Aries/1st), and therefore that his *own* emotional expression isn't going to be welcome.

His Pluto is in Libra/7th house and is square the nodes and Saturn. The soul's deepest intentions and wounding center on issues of fairness, harmony and balance in relationship. With the square to Saturn on the South Node, we could imagine scenarios in which the demands of family and history drive change in his routes to learning about life through relationship. One example that could fit is that family expectations regarding his choice of mate prevent him in some lives from being with the mate of his choice, leaving him feeling disempowered when it comes to relationship, or many other things. Whatever the scenario, he has been left with the emotional impact that life is unfair, and beliefs that other people don't listen to him, there's no fairness in relationship, etc.

Related to the issue with which he came in for a session, his propensity to view life as unfair and through an emotional lens lead to his continuing temper tantrums well into adulthood. His conditioned beliefs brought him to decide there was no value in growing up (because if you do live as a Saturn figure), you will be hard and cold and not allow for honest emotional expression), and so he persisted in childish behavior.

In the years since we worked together, he has turned those attitudes around fully. He also has a Capricorn Moon, which tells us that he needs to be Saturnian in order to be happy (Moon is a signifier of happiness), and his North Node is in the 10th house (indicating a need to develop a stable, mature place in his society, and to be recognized for a work, which requires Saturnian commitment and sacrifice to achieve). When he began to take responsibility for his attitudes and behaviors, Saturn energy was no longer something for other people to use seemingly only to make his life difficult. It became clear to him it was a way of being for him to explore that provides him with much satisfaction. He has in many ways become a wonderful example to others of a responsible and humane use of Saturnian energy, and can therefore teach others new things about finding and developing new levels of maturity and responsibility.

Toward the beginning of this process, I prescribed daily exercise for him to give something for the 1st house Mars-Chiron in Aries something to do. I knew that he would not find his way to and through Saturn/Capricorn in healthy ways if the physical energy he carried in his body was not being moved on a regular basis. The long-term work called for by Saturn can be derailed if we are not comfortable sitting still and focusing on tasks. Taking responsibility for this alleviated his perceived need for his abundant physical energy (Mars in Aries/1st) to come out in the form of emotional explosiveness. It was a Saturnian move and helped him see how to create structure for emotional expression and come out of the lingering sense of immaturity that was no longer serving him. When I speak with him now, it is sometimes a little difficult to believe he is the same person and he ends up showing me about healthy and proactive uses of Saturnian energy!

Client Chart 2, Female
December 6 1975, 4:08 PM, Newark OH

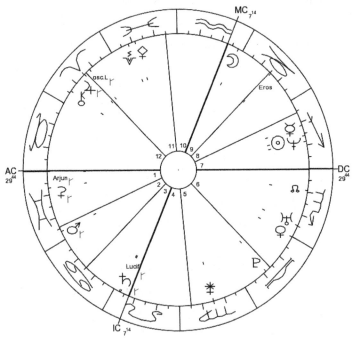

Life Issue: This woman lives on the West Coast and has a large extended family in the Midwest. She and her husband plan to begin having children soon, and they receive regular promptings from the Midwest family members that they should move back to be closer to the family once they do. The Midwest contingent paints a picture of blissful connectedness, which serves both as a seductive tease and repeated pressure. This pressure is difficult, as she knows the good that can come of having numerous family members nearby, yet she knows she needs to be individuated and live in a place of her own choosing.

Relevant Chart Configurations:

1. South Node in Taurus/12th house
2. SN ruler Venus in Libra/6th house, conjunct Uranus in Scorpio/6th house
3. North Node in Scorpio/6th house

The South Node is in the 12th house. This speaks of a karmic history of going with the flow. The house related to Neptune and Pisces asks us to give up our sense of individuality in order to fit in to the greater whole or reality that surrounds us. It calls for sacrifice. When the South Node is in the 12th, it is common to find that the person has been conditioned to notice the flow around him or herself and then learn to adapt to it. In the 12th house there is a lot of either willing sacrifice of individual interests in order to fit in, or a sacrifice of them in order to survive.

With the South Node ruler Venus in Libra, the woman has a karmic history of roles defined by listening to others first, to being a person who takes others' desires and needs into account before her own (or, at least, as much as her own). Libra is the sign of exploring fairness in relationship, which can lead one to spending a lot of energy making others happy, and defining the self in terms of how we understand others; we know our identity and place because we know ourselves in terms of our relationships with others. When Libra as a method is overdone, resentment can build and lead to aggression: We give too much power to others...*until we don't*, which can signal an end to our willingness to negotiate and collaborate. Libra is the sign of learning what fairness and harmony are, and the path to this learning can involve forgoing our sense of trusting that it is okay to take initiative on our own, without taking others and their desires and needs into account.

This South Node ruler Venus is in the 6th house, the house of duty and service. The 6th house often shows up in the karmic story when a person finds it is more useful to act from a sense of duty instead of desire or passion. The 6th house represents parts of life where we take responsibility for making something better by devoting ourselves to service, and this can at times involve sacrificing our sense of uniqueness and individuality. With the South Node ruler in the 6th, we can expect this person to know how to be a great team player and pitch in where and when she is needed, even if part of her resents it. She has been trained to live in the 6th house, a hands-on, nose-on-grindstone kind of place.

Venus is conjunct Uranus in Scorpio, also in the 6th house. The range of possible Uranian expression is from utterly free to utterly bored (some of us don't break out of constricting scenarios when filled with Uranian energy until the dam breaks). With Uranus conjunct the South Node ruler, she is being conditioned by trying to figure out the right way to use Uranian energy in her many lives. *How much freedom is sufficient? How much is enough?* are some questions that will come up for her. She is going to be very familiar with the Uranian impulses, but might not feel that she gets to express the energy for her own health and to her own benefit.

South Node ruler Venus and Uranus are in a T-square with Moon in Aquarius/9th house and Saturn-rx Lucifer in Leo/3rd house. This indicates pressure from family (Moon) and authority figures (Saturn-Lucifer) to change. The effect can be a feeling of pulled by the demands and needs of each kind of person or group, and at times caught in the middle. Saturn energy in a square has the quality of heavy expectations patiently waiting for us to surrender. Adding Lucifer to Saturn square the South Node ruler adds the energy of doubt to her own sense of embodying Saturn energy, potentially leaving even more apparent reasons to give in to the expectations of her family members.

The pull she feels between connectedness to family and her sense of freedom has been going on in many lives. In fact, it's probable that it was with this same family group in at least some of them. As her karma involves different levels of sacrifice to the desires and will of the family system (SN ruler Venus in Libra/6th), they will expect her to remain in or return to the Midwest before or when she begins having children. Her task now is to feel what is right for her and to trust this, and then decide from a healthy Uranian place of choosing more freedom, rather than making decisions from within the confines of the desires of others. She has arrived at the point where she has clarity that sacrificing her will and making decisions based in others' definitions of duty and service no longer brings her fulfillment.

Her North Node is in Scorpio in the 6th house indicates a need to get to the bottom (Scorpio) of what duty and sacrifice (6th house) really are. She needs to uncover the truth about what's worth sacrificing, and perhaps more importantly, what isn't. Scorpio's said to be about intensity and it is, but the basic idea behind this is that it is willing to dig down into things to find truth on deeper levels. In fact, it needs to. As she gains confidence that her reasons for staying on the West Coast are valid and what it is that she should do for her own development, she'll have to dig into each reason she feels she should or shouldn't move back to gain a true understanding of the real purpose and place of duty and sacrifice.

Client Chart 3, Female
September 15 1974, 3:59 PM, Upland CA

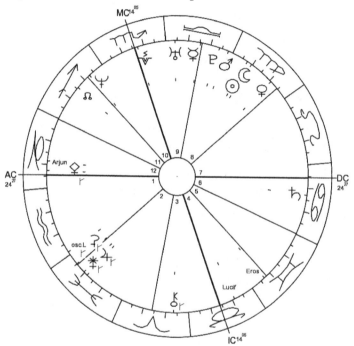

Life Issue: This woman felt she needed to develop her side business on a full-time basis and leave her full-time office employment, as it felt like it was getting her nowhere. She was confronting fears that she wouldn't be successful doing it, even though it made her significantly more happy than the other jobs she had had over the years. It felt to her more like a career than anything else she had done.

Relevant Chart Configurations:

1. Jupiter in Pisces/2nd and Venus in Virgo/8th square the nodal axis
2. SN ruler Mercury in Libra/9th square Saturn in Cancer/6th
3. Neptune conjunct the Sagittarius/11th house North Node
4. Pluto-Mars in Libra/8th house

The squares to her nodal axis indicate unresolved issues around learning how much faith she can have in herself (Jupiter in Pisces/2nd) versus how much value she should put in the opinions of trusted others (opposing Venus in Virgo/8th). The situation centered on her self-worth. The question of if she would make it being self-employed seemed to me to boil down to whether she was willing to believe in her abilities, even when they seem or are said by others to be imperfect. (This did not happen in reality. Others appreciate her work and find her very good at what she does.)

Jupiter square the nodes says that in this soul's lives it is exploring how much faith to have, how much risk to take, and how expansive to be. Venus square the nodes says that the soul is learning about how to choose the right people for relationships, which is in turn a statement of learning about developing an appropriate value system (our associates reflect what is important to us). The opposition of these two bodies square the nodes shows an argument. The back-and-forth between them in her psyche is the result of emotional pain after choices made in various lives about how much self-worth to have and who can be trusted. It can perpetuate itself by feeding her reasons to feel poorly about herself.

The SN ruler Mercury squares Saturn in Cancer in the 6th house. This aspect is about learning about authority in various lives by feeling knocked off center by Saturnian others. They could and will include those more experienced than she is, or those older, or those who just *seem* better or more experienced than she is at a given task. It can manifest as direct criticism from such people, or it can be that she observes the skills and competencies of others and assumes that they are more qualified, experienced, or competent than she is. Note that the squares to the nodal axis reflect the groundwork for this kind of expectation. She carries a belief that she's not good enough, and will be inclined to assume it is the truth, yet the truth is that it has a lot to do with having listened to the wrong people (i.e., not herself).

Neptune conjunct the North Node indicates that she needs in this life to recapture the willingness to go with the flow, to trust in the big picture, and to surrender to something. The karmic knot from her soul's various lives is not getting to "do Neptune," for some reason not getting to surrender or trust in the big picture (whether blocked specifically or prevented by circumstance). When she does trust in this life, she can take the argument between Jupiter and Venus squaring the nodes for what it is — differing opinions – instead of a valid statement about her worth. She can feel connected to a greater sense of reality than simply pitting her ideas of her worth versus the ideas of others.

Pluto and Mars are conjunct in Libra/8th house. The soul's deepest desires and wounding are wrapped up with the expression of will, and they are in the sign of interacting with others and trying to learn moderation. These two in the 8th house and Libra speak to a soul-level intention of transforming with other people in the most intense areas of life. Pluto in Libra seeks to do the most important things with other people. It is a placement of majoring in relationships in a bigger way than are most humans. Pluto in Libra people might wait for a trusted other in order to get on with what they are most passionate about, and this karmic signature in addition to Venus in Virgo/8th squaring the nodes says that the soul needs to heal an ability to trust others and learn that she can truly trust others only if she trusts herself. Choosing on her own to do work she loves is healing for the part of her that strongly values the opinions and feedback of others.

When she does that work, she in fact has more opportunity to confront the parts of her that feel she might not be good enough, and change the karma regarding self-worth by choosing to let those opinions go. Because it is true that she does good work, her success will hinge upon whether or not she is willing to let the positive reflections of others be more true than the inner voices of doubt.

Client Chart 4, Female
April 17 1953, 8:05 PM, Orlando FL

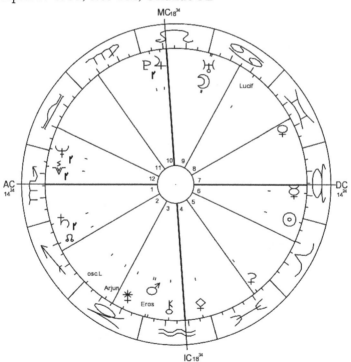

Life Issue: Much of her adult experience has been defined by her marriage. When the marriage was under stress she became very aware of this, and sought ways to step out on her own, develop her own friendships and social outlets, and give herself more of a voice and social presence outside the definition of her marriage.

Relevant Chart Configurations:

1. SN in Gemini/7th conjunct Venus, rx Saturn conjunct the Sagittarius/1st NN

2. SN ruler Mercury square Mars-Eros and Chiron in Aquarius/3rd house

3. NN ruler Jupiter conjunct rx Pluto in Leo/10th

Her South Node is in Gemini/7th and conjunct Venus. This tells of a karmic history of learning a lot about what it takes to make relationships work. She has become a professional at being aware of what is happening with others and adapting either to their needs or the needs of the relationship (Gemini calls for flexibility). With Venus there, courtesy is a valued aspect of these environments. Kindness and graceful approaches to others are important. Diplomacy is key. Listening to others is understood as the way to making relationships work.

The SN ruler Mercury is in Taurus in the 6th house. In the context of these environments, her role has to do with taking responsibility (6th) for how things are going. Taurus indicates that she is deliberate and works with intention, and probably isn't going to be rushed through anything, letting things take the time they need.

Mercury is squared both by Mars-Eros and Chiron in Aquarius/3rd. In various lives has been pushed off course or caught off guard by, or in some other way received friction from, different sorts of Aquarian energy. As both Aquarius and squares from Mars can indicate sudden events and even violence that results in trauma, for her to fully bring out this Aquarius/3rd house energy she will be confronted with the challenges of healing any hesitancy to fully express Mars and Eros energy that might be sourced in trauma. As these are in the 3rd house, how she thinks and what is on her mind are full of this energy.

Chiron also there indicates a sensitivity to the pain and suffering of others. From her environment she will absorb signals of others' difficulties in their voices and bodies, in the words they choose, how they walk, etc. Being sensitive to the pain of others may make someone with this placement hesitant to speak boldly, much or often, knowing the kinds of information that she picks up around her could wound others, yet others could also pick up such information from her. Karmically speaking, this could be experienced as hurtful words directed at her that made her stop and think before she spoke freely, and then think some more, and then more, until she was more quiet than anything else, terrified of hurting others.

The NN is in Sagittarius in the 1st house conjunct retrograde Saturn. This speaks of a need to develop independence and a sense of adventure, to become willing to take risks in order to be re-energized about life, to reorient toward prioritizing her intuitions to her own needs instead of the needs of others. Retrograde Saturn conjunct the NN says that in her various lives she does not get to learn about how to embody the energy of discipline, structure, authority, and hard work. That it is retrograde says that she has to figure out her own versions of Saturn energies. She will be surrounded by people who comfortable embodying different sides of Saturnian energy, yet none of the examples or models will work for her. Her husband embodies Saturnian energy, and it has been easy for her to let him do it for the both of them for a long time until she felt the need to begin developing it in herself.

The NN ruler Jupiter is in the 10th house in Leo conjunct retrograde Pluto. One way to really get inside this North Node (other than consciously choosing to focus on developing a healthy relationship with her Saturn conjunct the NN) is to focus on Jupiter, the sign's ruler. It is conjunct her deepest soul intentions and desires, wrapped up in her soul's empowerment journey, so doing this will call her to confront the Plutonian pain and fear she may have about standing up in public in any way. Pluto in the 10th house symbolizes a wound to the expression of ambition, and to the experience of creating a positive place for ourselves in our community, society or culture. Because these are part and parcel of the soul's deepest intentions and desires, figuring out this Jupiter (or Saturn) will prove deeply fulfilling for her, aligning her with what her soul came here to do. Remember also that the 10th house is Saturn's house, and it is easy to see how Plutonian wounding in the 10th could lead a person to avoid embodying a 1st house Saturn.

Client Chart 5, Female
December 1 1975, 5:24 PM, Hartford CT

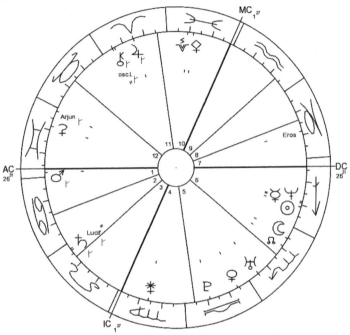

Life Issue: This woman came to me about relationship issues. She was separated from her husband, and wanted to know if they should get back together. It was her choice to separate after the relationship turned abusive in one way. At the same time he was also spending a lot of time with and having what seemed to be an emotional involvement with another woman. During the separation she saw another man with whom she had much more chemistry and connection than with her husband, but the man wanted her to take care of him financially and in other ways she refused to do, and he had a history of addiction to pornography. She wanted to talk about the men she was attracting.

Relevant Chart Configurations:

1. Moon conjunct North Node
2. South Node ruler Venus opposing retrograde true Black Moon and retrograde Chiron in Aries/11th and square retrograde Saturn and retrograde Lucifer in Leo/2nd
3. Pluto in Libra/5th

Her South Node is in the 12th house, which speaks to a history of going with the flow. Her Moon is conjunct the North Node, indicating that taking care of her own needs and making herself happy something she is not accustomed to doing. The people she comes from (the environments) did not teach her to do this. This combination says that forces greater than her required for one reason or another that happiness be sacrificed for what was perceived to be the greater good. She will be unsure in this life whether she gets to make herself happy, and probably will repeatedly throw her hands up in the air when confronted with the necessity of taking care of herself, having little idea of how to do it or why it should be done. Moon energy is lacking in the environments of her various lives – happiness and meeting her own needs are not happening for the people in places from which she comes (family of origin, etc.). They are not taught by their forebears about this part of life so do not know how to do it healthily and as a consequence, they will share an unhappiness among them.

The South Node ruler Venus is in Libra in the 5th house, opposing Lilith and Chiron in Aries/11th. Her role in her various lives is as the peacemaker, mediator, artist, and lover. She is defined by these attitudes and behaviors, and she is the one in her relationships willing to bend over backwards to make things work and keep the peace. The opposition to Chiron-Lilith in Aries/11th says that in her various lives she is opposed by hurt and angry groups of people. As I studied her chart before she came in for her session I had the image of an angry mob (Lilith-Chiron in Aries/11th) striking her down for expressing too much sensuality or sexuality through some art form (opposing Venus in Libra/5th). This opposition functions in her family system, as her Egyptian family doesn't approve of the idea of her pursuing acting, her chosen profession.

Part of her familial energetic inheritance is an anger against women, but more generally the feminine. Her personal experience of this can be seen in the Chiron-Lilith in Aries opposing her role (Venus). The long-seeded suppression of the feminine in her Egyptian heritage came out in her family of origin as rage from her father. It resulted in abuse of her and her mother. Her father channeled in unhealthy ways the pain and anger at the abuse of the wild (uncontrollable) feminine that he inherited from his family.

Karmically, she believes in this party line adopted by the family. She chose this family not just because she had karmic business with them, but also because she needs at the soul level to make peace with the cultural mores about sexuality, sexual expression and sensuality that run through her ancestral lines. When she has found herself not honored for being who she is, she has assumed that she does not deserve to be and express herself fully. Consequently her ability to create healthy relationships depends on her willingness to stop believing that this (and anything like it) is true.

The man she saw during her separation offered her a chance to have a relationship with a high sexual charge, as well as a lot of chemistry and compatibility. This was a wonderful experience for her. He treated her like a queen, and this also was important to shaking her out of past patterns. Yet he also had an addiction to pornography and expected her to help him take care of himself in ways she was clear she would not do (organizing and taking care of his finances is one example). This fits with her need to learn more about balancing relationship with equality. The conditioned belief that she cannot have a relationship that really works for her if she expresses who she really is was ready to be unraveled. The addiction to pornography was an echo to her father's and ancestors' attitudes about women, and the key to unraveling each was the same: 1) *Unlearning the notion that she does not get to have relationships in which she is treated as an equal* **and** *honored for exactly who she really is, 2) Releasing the expectation that if she shows herself, she'll be abused, or ignored or overlooked, and 3) Giving herself permission to move into creating relationships that provide the opportunity for happiness, healthy expression of self and sexuality.* Along the way, this will require her to give up the meaning attached to her memories of abuse and inequality, namely that she does not deserve to have relationships with men that work well and serve and honor her.

All that said, her Pluto in Libra in the 5th speaks to the soul-level need to express herself and be heard as an individual. Creativity of course serves this need, but the underlying idea is to express herself and to be heard, to show others who she really is and have that be acknowledged, and to form relationships based on who she really is, not what others might expect of her or want to think of her. All of what is written above feeds and supports her soul's need to learn to create relationships that are based in harmony, equality and fairness. She began to act on her unhappy feelings about her marriage when Pluto transited her Descendant a few years prior. The reality of the marriage relationship could no longer be ignored. Its transit through her 7th house is giving her numerous chances to revisit these karmic issues and to learn about her next levels of healthy relating.

Client Chart 6, Female
June 29 1967, 10:31 PM, Oxford OH

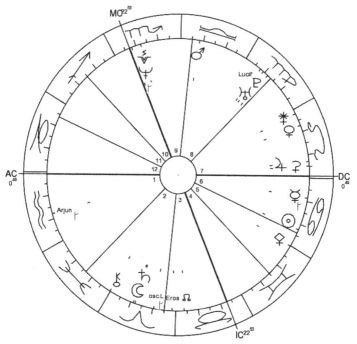

Life Issue: This woman came to me as a student, and after a couple of tutoring sessions had a session with me. It was based on questions and concerns about her learning style and memories of numerous difficult experiences in her education that had left their mark on her willingness to have confidence in her skills and self. She is bright, eager to learn, and passionate about learning new skills, and wanted to overcome the memories that made her feel that she had little reason to have confidence in herself.

Relevant Chart Configurations:

1. South Node in Scorpio/9th, North Node in Taurus/3rd
2. SN ruler Mars in Libra/9th square retrograde Mercury in Cancer/6th
3. North Node ruler Mercury retrograde in Cancer/6th.
4. Pluto-Uranus-Lucifer in Virgo/8th opposing retrograde Chiron in Pisces/2nd

The South Node is in Scorpio in the 9th house. Her environments in various lives have a lot to do with seeking information and exploring what is true. She has been conditioned to value digging for the truth, being empowered by digging below the surface, and understanding what is to be found under various rocks. One way to look at this is that she is an expert at going on long journeys of various kinds in order to seek and root out the truth. The North Node in Taurus/3rd indicates that she hasn't done a lot of in her various lives, what feels foreign to her, is a slow and methodical exploration of what is actually happening in her environment. The 3rd-9th axis is about how we gather and process information. In the 9th house, we pick what seems the most true to us and go in search of supporting data, or we intuit and feel into the direction we think the truth resides and head toward it. In this house we can have an idea of what we are looking for and then evaluate all data coming our way in terms of fitting them in with our idea. In the 3rd, we explore our environment, taking in a lot of sensory data, and allow ourselves to be changed by it. We learn about the world around us by observing, touching, tasting, and listening. This woman is practiced in the search for truth, yet unpracticed in simply taking what is around her and using it to learn about the world.

The South Node ruler Mars in Libra/9th is squared by retrograde Mercury in Cancer/6th, speaking to her in various lives receiving friction from methodical Mercurial sources. How she has experienced this in this life is as criticism for her natural learning style (Libra/9th is highly intuitive and not often grounded). The evolutionary intention is to drive her to the challenge of trusting herself, trusting how she knows she needs to approach learning.

In our first conversation, before she began lessons with me, one of her major concern was that she would not be served by how the lessons were designed, leaving her to experience another instance of deeply wanting to learn, yet not feeling open to do it her way and to explore the material the way she needs to. I assured her that all of my lessons are geared toward not just what the student wants to learn but also to *how* he or she learns, and she was encouraged by this. I offered her the chance to either devise what we would do or, because I knew her Mercury was retrograde and Chiron is in her 2nd house, related to issues of confidence about learning and her skills, to edit a plan of my choosing into one that she felt would suit her best. She opted for the latter, and the lessons have turned out several different ways. We check in periodically about what she wants to do, and this kind of interaction allows her to have the kind of input she needs to heal this karmic debris about learning and self-confidence. She can then use this Mars-Mercury square to help drive her curiosity and to figure out new routes to learning instead of experiencing them as an unhappy friction that comes out as criticism of how she learns, both being normal expressions of the square.

Reading Mercury on another level as the planet associated with the NN house, it represents a route to learning Taurus/3rd house ways of being. The planet's placement in Cancer means that it works through what could be called an emotional lens. The way her mind works will always include the input of emotional information, both from her and from other people. That it is retrograde means that she needs to figure out her own way to do Mercury. Others' ideas of learning/education and communication simply will not work for her. She can adopt others' ideas of how to do these things all she wants, but in the end they simply cannot serve her except as examples of what does not work for her. The bottom line is that her mind works differently. The real task for her is to be willing to explore different means of and routes to learning and communication but more importantly, to learn to trust herself along the way. I see the key for her on these issues is learning to trust that her learning style is valid, and that she has the right to develop self-confidence even if she is different.

This is a great segue in to treating Pluto-Uranus-Lucifer in Virgo/8th opposing Chiron in Pisces/2nd. The deepest soul wound she carries has to do with trusting people, but really in trusting herself to choose the right people to trust. Pluto-Uranus together want to evolve by finding new routes to creating freedom, but Lucifer in the mix says that experience has lead her to doubt her ability to do so. Chiron in Pisces in the 2nd is about a wound to the willingness to surrender to the perfection of herself as she is. The 2nd house is about self-confidence and self-reliance, and this Chironic wounding says that she has a differentness, a uniqueness in how she goes about gathering and using skills and resources. These energies in opposition will lead her to an inner argument about whom she can trust if she can trust anyone at all. With this configuration, she can spend a lot of time finding reasons (through her sensitivity to what is happening inside other people about their own self-worth) to doubt her own worth. The more she learns to trust herself and the perfection of how she is wired, the more her unique way of learning (retrograde Mercury) can be given space to flourish.

Client Chart 7, Female
February 3 1974, 12:57 PM, Nashville TN

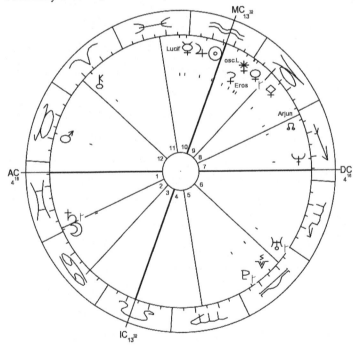

Life Issue: She was confronting a fear of not being respected at work, while knowing she was equal to her peers.

Relevant Chart Configurations:

1. Saturn-Moon conjunct the Gemini South Node, North Node in Sagittarius/7th

2. South Node ruler Mercury conjunct Lucifer in Pisces/10th square the Ascendant/Descendant axis and Neptune in Sagittarius/7th

With the South Node in Gemini, she has been conditioned to open up to her environment and learn what it can teach her. Gemini is the lens of the zodiac always open for new information to become available because everything could be different when that new information is factored in. In other words, Gemini does not want to make a stand about what is true but wants to continually explore and gather new data.

With Saturn-Moon conjunct this South Node, these energies saturate the environments she keeps finding herself in various lives. A structured approach to emotional expression and meeting one's needs is one way this can manifest. A dedication to work on behalf of family and related issues is another. Whatever it is, she is carrying into this life much understanding about Saturn-Moon aspects of life. All of this is taking place in the 1st house, which means that she is strongly conditioned by environments shaped by leadership, the need to make quick decisions, and instinct.

Her North Node in Sagittarius/7th tells us that this chapter of her journey involves a lot learning about sharing with other people and intuitively opening to learn to create fair and balanced relationships. A huge part of this will mean learning to listen to others and developing a willingness to trust what they reflect to her. While the South Node in Gemini tells us she is a pro at gathering data, the use of that data will be for 1st house ends, and it is in the 7th house that one learns about what it takes to be in relationship with others. Having faith in others and what they have to share and offer is one way to approach this North Node.

The South Node ruler Mercury is in Pisces/10th and conjunct the asteroid Lucifer. This tells me that her role in various lives centers on taking an idea of service into her work and therefore the world. She is accustomed to creating for herself a place in society that allows her to serve a greater good (both Pisces and Lucifer speak to this). That it is conjunct Lucifer however brings in the voice of doubt. Her memories of her various lives include doubting that she gets to express this 10th house energy and doubt that she can get respect for what she does in the public sphere. It is likely that she has had experiences in various lives of being labeled in some way or received feedback that she is egotistical or self-centered (keywords for negative Lucifer). She will have in many ways taken these to be valid judgments of herself, so she will doubt that what she wants to do in 10th house scenarios is worth pursuing or that she is doing it for the right reasons.

The issue she presented regarded scenarios at work as an attorney working for a non-profit focused on animal rights. She doubted that she should express herself with a high level of confidence to the other executives there. She believes in what she does and is passionate about it, yet in this particular scenario she doubts her ability to have authority or to be authoritative. She is saturated with Saturnian energy, but karmically she has experienced sides of Saturn energy that leave her with undermined confidence (receiving criticism, etc.).

The healing route for her was to change her mind that only other people get to be Saturnian (respected, authoritative, etc.) and to heal her tendency to doubt that what she has to say and how she says it (Mercury-Lucifer in the 10th) are important. Healing the Lucifer issue requires checking in with her true motivation and then trusting that in order to give her greatest gift (to bring the light), she has to be clear about her motivation and then trust herself to act on it. When we do our Lucifers, we run the risk of being labeled arrogant and self-serving, but we must learn to trust that acting with enlightened self-interest does in fact enable us to do what we came here to do.

This is a great example of a soul that is very familiar with an energy, but for karmic growth it needs to learn new things about that energy. In her case, there is a resonance with the conjunction of Saturn to her South Node and the South Node ruler being in Saturn's house, the 10th. She comes in with much experience of Saturn, but is challenged to become an authority figure as part of her karmic growth. With her, the old belief is that other people get to be Saturnian in positive ways while she gets to experience Saturn as heavy and burdensome and always asking for hard work and commitment (which she is very comfortable with). The default that she is changing is that as soon as she has the opportunity to stand up and receive respect for her work, a part of her doubts that she should.

Client Chart 8, Female

August 20 1959, 7:15 PM, Dorchester MA

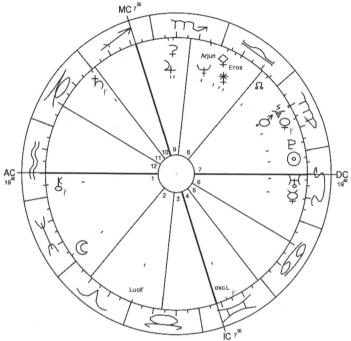

Life Issue: After many years as a hands-on healer, this woman decided to make a change and obtained her real estate license. In a work situation at this time she found herself supporting a colleague in his work where the boundaries were not healthy and she was left feeling that she might have made a series of mistakes in choosing that path.

Relevant Chart Configurations:

1. SN conjunct Moon in Pisces/1ˢᵗ

2. SN ruler Mars in Virgo/7ᵗʰ opposing Moon in Pisces/1ˢᵗ

3. Rx Saturn in Capricorn/11th square the nodal axis
4. Pluto in Virgo/7th conjunct Sun in Leo/7th and opposing rx Chiron in Aquarius/1st

With the Pisces Moon conjunct the 1st house South Node, this woman comes from environments with a focus on Lunar issues. Emotional realities, issues of family, belonging, connectedness, and security will be emphasized in them. This would predispose someone to the inner workings of others, as a Pisces Moon can indicate a psychic sensitivity and energetic/emotional porousness. The South Node ruler Mars is in Virgo in the 7th, indicating experience with taking responsibility for what is happening in relationship. Her role in various lives is as a Virgo figure in the realm of other people, and work as a healer is certainly a kind of real-world manifestation of this energy.

Mars is opposed by a retrograde Chiron in Aquarius/1st. Confronting her in various lives is the woundedness and trauma of others. She will manifest Chironic, wounded others in various lives and have to make a choice about how to respond. What a Pisces Moon and Chiron have in common is a sensitivity to the energetic and emotional realities of others. Her choice to be a healer in response to what she witnessed and felt around her is just one kind of choice. She could just as easily have responded by shutting down, by trying to lessen the influx of emotional and energetic information coming her way by some form of escapist behavior that took her out of conscious awareness of it and offered the promise of numbness or escape. Very Chironic and Neptunian people can find themselves responding to the suffering and pain of other people to the point that they cease to consider their own desires. Some of them get wrapped up in the crises and healing of others and stop making choices for themselves. They ask themselves, *Who am I if can feel the pain of others and do nothing about it? What kind of person would that make me?*

This woman in various lives has done just that, and her growth requires dealing with the unresolved issue of that retrograde Saturn in Capricorn/11th squaring the nodes. Her soul is trying to figure out the right place of work (Saturn square the nodes) and what it really means to be mature and responsible (Saturn retrograde). In the 11th house, this is about where work gets her. The 11th is on one level about creating the future we want to live in, and to navigate it well we have to choose the right people and groups to work with to make that happen, as none of us can create the future we want on our own. In her case, she has been committed to work that has not gotten her where she needs to go for soul growth. This retrograde Saturn presents her with an invitation to learn to make new choices about what she does for a living and how that contributes to the kind of future she wants to live.

She manifested the difficult situation at work with the other real estate professional to reflect her own hidden assumptions about what happens when she makes new choices about what do to for a living, as well as some 7th house Pluto fairness issues. If you are committed to doing healing work and feel that you are giving all of yourself in the spirit of service to others, you might develop opinions about people in business for profit who seem not to be helping others in the ways that you are.[12] To someone devoted to being a healer, a profession like real estate might seem worthless. In her reading I told her it did not matter if her new choice was real estate or running a hot dog stand or anything else, but the choice to do something new that broke with her history of being single-minded about work was the important issue.

Pluto in Virgo/7th conjunct the Sun in Leo/7th and opposing the 1st house Chiron in Aquarius will come into play in all of her work, no matter the profession. Her soul-based questions about her part in creating fairness and harmony in relationship (Pluto in Virgo/7th) is joined with a need to express herself in

---

[12] The truth about work is that none is any better than another, but along our soul journeys as humans we can formulate all sorts of opinions about what work means, who does what, and why it is and should be done.

relationship and to understand herself in terms of them (Sun in Leo/7th). Chiron in Aquarius/1st in opposition to these says that she will always be aware of the subtle emotional and energetic undercurrents that underlie all of her interactions. As a healer, this is an invaluable skill as she supports others in healing issues of which they might not even be conscious. As a business person, this will inform all of her dealings with colleagues and clients and support her in developing success in that new kind of work.

Her karma involves believing that she should be a healer. Making a new choice in any professional direction can be a route to healing the debris from the past made up of judgments about what different kinds of work mean about the people who do them.

Client Chart 9, Female

Life Issue: The youngest of several children, for most of her life her family behaved as if she did not exist or that they would rather she did not. She was always viewed as unworthy of positive attention. By the time we first spoke she had already recognized that this informed the romantic relationships of her adulthood and wanted to work through the issues.

Relevant Chart Configurations:

1. SN in Scorpio/4th conjunct rx Neptune
2. True Black Moon Lilith in Aquarius/7th square the nodal axis

3. Rx Pluto in Virgo/2ⁿᵈ opposing Saturn-Chiron in Pisces/8ᵗʰ

4. Venus in Aquarius/6ᵗʰ inconjunct Pluto

March 21 1966, 2:41 PM, Alton IL

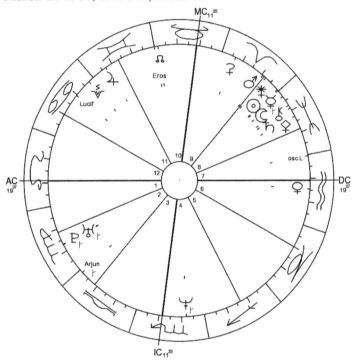

With the SN in Scorpio/4ᵗʰ, in various lives her soul is learning about Scorpionic ways of connecting to others. It is a marker of the intention to delve deeply into the inner realities of what makes one tick, which will include intense relationships with family members. In this life this woman has experienced a lot of the negative sides of Scorpio energy while growing up, yet she is also capable of honest work on her inner self that might make some other people shrink away (some courageous Scorpionic/4th house work).

Neptune conjunct the SN says that the Neptune is at the core of that inner landscape and her relationships with family. Healthy explorations of Neptune can serve to answer her questions about the people she comes from yet in her particular family system, Neptune is manifested as denial and escapism, seeking to avoid the truth. One example is that the family picture was intentionally not retaken after she was born (the youngest of several children), so she grew up looking at a picture of the family on the mantle that did not include her.

Her karma includes the true Black Moon Lilith square the nodal axis from Aquarius in the 7th house. Her environments in various lives, including this family, have an unresolved issue how to accept the energy of the wild in the form of other people. Lilith in Aquarius needs us to allow our natural selves to be expressed as, how and when they wish; to honor the natural flow of our uniqueness and to remove all limitations to experiencing ourselves as extensions of nature. In other words, this woman is conditioned in environments where other people who behave outside the norm are not understood and are far from accepted. The 7th house is where we encounter others and learn what it takes to form, exist in, and end relationships. The karmic imprint here is that if she behaves as she naturally feels she is wired to do, she will attract the kind of Saturnian sanction that Lilith people in our culture draw: various kinds of punishment and abuse for being uncontrollable.

On the personal level she needs to learn to accept her Lilith side and be willing to take it to other people. To resolve this issue, she will have to make peace with this part of herself and then be willing to choose friends and partners who are interested in working, living, and playing with a Lilith-inspired figure.

The square to the nodes says she needs to make new choices about the energy in question. The new choice here is in radical self-acceptance and creating a social network for herself that invites her to express herself fully. In the context of her family can see that they are all trying to deal with deeply-rooted Neptunian denial issues and cannot imagine what to do with a Lilith figure, other than to ignore or attempt to repress her, both of which she experienced in her relationships with them.

Retrograde Pluto in Virgo/2nd (conjunct rx Uranus) speaks to a soul intention and desire to learn discrimination in the arena of self-worth. As Pluto-Uranus are opposed to Saturn-Chiron in Pisces/8th, her intention and wound are wrapped up in an awareness of the sensitivity of others and the need to take cues from her most important relationships about her own self-worth. The phrase that comes to my mind for her with this is "consider the source." It is important to take reflection of herself from others, but she also needs to be picky about whom she chooses to receive reflections from. She was naturally shaped importantly by her experiences in her family, and her task now is to begin loving herself in all the ways she perceived she was not loved by her family (Pluto in the 2nd needs to focus on self-love and self-worth). Once she does that, she will be able to see with more clarity the kinds of people that are more appropriate for her to be and play with. The unresolved feelings about her family relationships can keep her from moving forward in other kinds of relationships, as she identified before calling me for a session.

It is important to note the inconjunct from Venus to Pluto-Uranus. This aspect echoes the symbolism of Lilith in Aquarius/7th squaring the nodes while adding a layer to the story about her history of exploring what it takes to create fairness and harmony in relationship. This symbol in the 6th house says there is an issue with inequality. We enter the 6th house to learn or teach something through experience or to serve, and there is naturally an imbalance of power in the relationships that fit here (mentoring, apprenticeship, and slavery are some of the possibilities). The inconjunct speaks to a soul need to be knocked off course by relationship. The ideal is in learning through experience to repeatedly re-orient styles of relating and ways of choosing others with whom to be in relationship. Making peace with her family relationships and acknowledging what they might be serving to teach her will free up inner space to help her get a handle on how she can go about her adult relationships in new ways and for new reasons.

Client Chart 10, Female
May 25 1943, 3:29 PM, Peoria IL

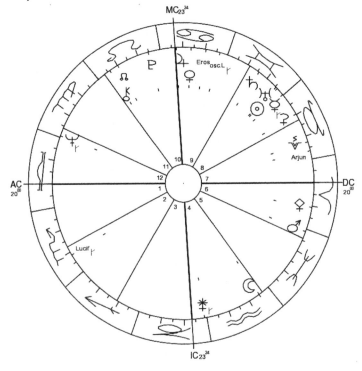

Life Issue: Finding the right kind of work after years of finding herself in difficult power plays in work situations.

Relevant Chart Configurations:

1. SN in the 4th house conjunct Moon
2. Chiron in Leo on the 10th house NN
3. Pluto in Leo/10th

With the SN in the 4th, this woman has lives being defined by the people she comes from, who she is at home, and who she is on the inside when no one else is around. She conditioned to consider her family relationships first as well as who she is in terms of them. The Moon conjuncting the SN emphasizes this strongly.

Her NN is in Leo in the 10th house. This speaks to a need to go out into the world and create a place for herself in it (or community, society, etc.) that allows her to express herself personally and that allows her to be seen in Leo ways and receive personal attention for her public persona and work. Chiron in Leo is conjunct the NN, indicating that establishing a place for herself in the world that is alternative (a Chiron keyword) and allows for her personal expression is not something she is very experienced at in her various lives. The value in her lives is consistently placed on what is happening at home and inside her.

Yet her Pluto is also in Leo in the 10th house. Her soul's deepest intention and desire is to express itself through some kind of work in the world. It seeks to create a place in her community that allows her to make a personal mark and receive recognition for it. Her work experience for many years was in offices and teaching situations in which she was seen never to fit in and as a result treated poorly. This came from her Chironic-NN need to be perceived as different in her public way of living. It could be thought of as an evolutionary pressure to be in the world but find out that traditional ways of being in it will not work for her.

She will have to do something different with and through her work. Having difficult and painful experiences through her jobs are ways to force her to figure out a different path, a very Chiron thing to do. The key to all of it is accepting herself in all the ways that others will not, basic Chironic healing.

Three things in her work/community biography have served to meet this Chiron-NN need, which in turn support the Pluto in Leo/10th need. First, when her children were in elementary school, she volunteered for four years to teach a small group of students in her kids' classes Spanish language and Native American culture. It was a curriculum not offered by the school and served students in ways that the school couldn't see doing, both positive Chiron elements.

The second Chiron-NN in Leo/10th to note is that her family was one of the few Jewish families in the small community. Each year when the December holiday events were being planned in the schools, she came in to meet with the principal of the elementary school to do what she could to remind him of the separation of church and state to ensure the holiday festivities in the school were not infused with a lot of religion, which they always tended toward. She also volunteered in various classrooms to educate the teachers and kids about Judaism.

The third Chironic note on her work biography is that she ended up being self-employed. By creating the chance to call her own shots in her work, she began healing both the Chiron/NN need to express herself differently and the Pluto in Leo/10th need to empower herself in some kind of public way.

Client Chart 11, Male

January 9 1970, 11:58 AM, Cambridge MA

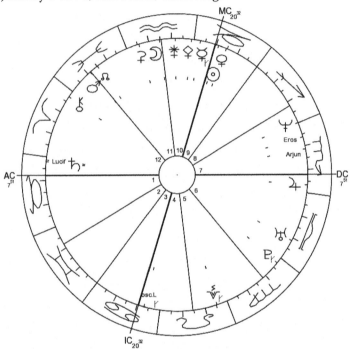

Life Issue: I met this man after he had done years of healing on past-life issues including deep anger. Recognizing that the source of the wounding was in other lives he had done much work with a psychic/intuitive healer to unearth past-life patterns to release them. He knew he has been in leadership positions in various lives, and has been dealing with the feelings lingering still from decisions he had made in such positions.

Relevant Chart Patterns:

1. SN ruler retrograde Mercury in Capricorn/10th, squared by Jupiter in Scorpio/6th and Saturn-Lucifer in Taurus/12th
2. Mars in Pisces conjunct the Pisces North Node
3. Retrograde Pluto in Virgo/6th

Mercury is retrograde in Capricorn in the 10th house. It is conjunct Pallas in Aquarius also in the 10th house. His role in various lives has him in the public sphere, doing things that require hard work and that get him respect for his expertise and leadership. Pallas Athene can show up in our lives as something we try to divorce ourselves from in order to be more successful by not making waves and fitting in. HIs 10th house role then will be something around which he works hard not to innovate (blocking Aquarian/10th house energy) to ensure he can be accepted by the prevailing majority.

When we are in the 10th house we become symbols for what we do in the world. In many lives he will identify to a great degree with his work function – who he is in public. Mercury is retrograde, which says that this role has been overdone and that in many lives he is performing this public role more because he can do so and it is needed, not necessarily because he is passionate about it. This is a signature of someone performing the public function of leadership who either does not really want to do it or who could use a break from it but does not refuse to do what he can for his community.

Mercury is involved in a t-square with Jupiter in Scorpio/6th and Saturn-Lucifer in Taurus/12th. The square to Jupiter says that in his public roles he is pressured by larger forces that are critical of his decisions (6th house) and can see through any pretense associated with his public persona (Scorpio). This could manifest at various times through self-righteous and powerful people trying to cut him down. The square to Saturn-Lucifer in Taurus/12th will manifest unmovable, powerful people or institutions to challenge him or to tell him he is not performing his role well.

In leadership positions, one must make decisions. If a leader makes decisions based in his or her conscience at some point or another he or she will encounter resistance from any established power structures to perceived attempts to change the status quo. Saturn represents authority, and Lucifer represents alignment to a higher power/truth (or lack of it). In Taurus this says that those authority figures are stubborn at best, unmovable at worst. The evolutionary intention of this t-square is to keep himself in check to ensure that he is serving well and for the right reasons yet there is wounding surrounding these experiences in various lives that needs to be healed before he would feel good about taking on leadership roles of any kind. The anger he carries is in part for being put into impossible situations, those in which he cannot possibly succeed given such pressures.

Mars conjunct the NN says that what is missing from his conditioning (and perceived options) has been to assert his own will. In Pisces on the cusp of the 12th house this alignment of will needs to be to a higher source. The Virgo SN says that control has been the name of the game and the Pisces NN says that it is time to surrender to a greater will, one outside of him. Consider the effect of this SN ruler Mercury, involved as he has been in public work and what his public persona can achieve. The standards of the cultures in which he finds himself are the prevailing context. Higher truth, or other worlds/dimensions/realms, have not always been in the picture. As an example, in most human cultures over the last few thousand years shaping public policy based in images and ideas you encounter in your nocturnal dreams is not something many public figures could admit to.

As a public figure, or via the work in the world with which he is deeply identified, he has been guided by a desire to serve (Pluto in Virgo/6th). His own will and personal desires have been sacrificed in order to serve his community and the world around him. And now it is time for him to reintegrate the energy of Mars, to claim for himself a sense of steering his own ship and to make sure that it reflects something higher. He needs to align his will with something more than his own ego.

This Mars on the NN is the other source of the anger, as he knows, even if unconsciously, that he deserves to express his desire and anger. Yet he has felt he is not someone with the luxury to do so – there is so much work to be done for the greater good, after all, who has time for petty grievances.

When his work in the world and/or leadership have brought him difficulty, he has been more inclined to take it as a reflection of his worth as a leader or role model. Overcoming this major part of his path to healing will require opening to this Pisces NN. It is a call for him to accept that there is an order to the Universe that we (he) cannot control and that events unfold in a way that reflects the unfolding of the Universe. Also good for him to learn is that there is a perfection in how things play out. When things go wrong we can take cues to learn about ourselves and how we fit into the greater scheme around us, letting go of the need to judge ourselves for our part in the greater plan.

Pluto in Virgo is the source of this entire story. The root desires and intentions of his soul have to do with serving and developing humility to create and offer something that will help people and make the world a better place. Virgo and the 6th house are each oriented toward the idea of perfection, and when things do not go well, people with Pluto in Virgo and/or the 6th might feel they didn't do enough, or didn't take on enough responsibility, or didn't do what they did do well enough. Karmic healing for this man would begin with forgiveness and compassion for himself.

Chapter 8: Celebrity Charts – Karma

This chapter looks at the charts and lives of a handful of well-known people as it explores various views into their karma and how it has shaped their lives. In most a specific issue is treated so we can see its root in the person's karmic history, whether that involves a symbol or two, or most or all of the chart.

Rosanna Arquette

Actress, Film Director & Producer
August 10 1959, 4:45 PM, New York NY

At her fortieth birthday, Arquette began to look at the effect aging would have on her career, recognizing that the standards of beauty in Hollywood are tied to youth, and that they prevent the existence of many quality roles for older actresses. She found herself also confronting the challenges of balancing home and family with a career in entertainment and set out to ask others in the same position about their experiences. She interviewed thirty-three actresses ages 30-60 about the realities of aging and maintaining a career in entertainment, which resulted in the documentary "Searching For Debra Winger," released in 2002.

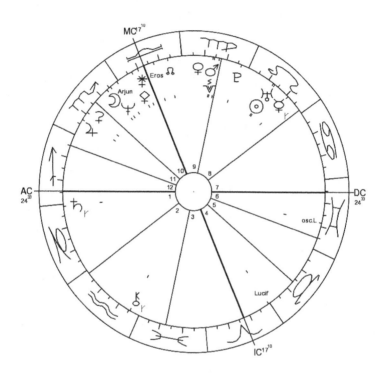

Arquette has retrograde Saturn in Capricorn in the 1st house square the nodal axis. This describes karma of having maturity, authority, competency and respect as unresolved issues. In the 1st, the issues are about her own personality and body, but really about how she inhabits and embodies maturity, competency, authority, and shows up as someone deserving of respect.

With this signature, the right relationship to work is a karmic issue for her. How much work to do, how much to identify with what one does, and how to develop into a person worthy of respect (but really self-respect) are some of the kinds of questions that can come up with this signature. Receiving challenges to one's competency could result, and also difficulties in developing into the kind of adult one wants to be.

That Saturn is retrograde says that whatever models of adult behavior presented to her, she needs to go her own way and develop into her own kind of adult. She might have in this or other lives, when young, adopted her family's ideas of what it means to be a responsible adult or competent leader. She would then grow up and find out via experience that it did not work for her, thereby needing to figure out new ways to live the energy of Saturn. Saturn is also about time, aging, and orienting toward reality even when difficult to deal with, and this planet values what is forged over time.

Taking this all together, "Searching For Debra Winger" seems the result of Arquette's process of asking and answering for herself questions about the realities of aging in her chosen line of work, and the challenge of becoming a leader concerning an issue related to Saturn. Creating a film that takes into account the experiences and opinions of other women in the same situation, she evidences leadership in an area that has had little leadership in the history of the industry. By answering her own questions of competency, and not allowing the realities of her industry change her opinion of herself, she had healed at least some of her karmic baggage related to this retro Saturn in Capricorn in the 1st squaring the nodal axis.

David Bowie

Musician, Actor

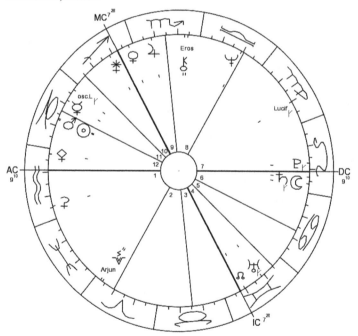

January 8 1947, 9:15 AM, Brixton England (rated AA)

David Bowie has his South Node (SN) in Sagittarius in the 10th house conjunct Juno in the same sign and

211

house. It is also conjunct Venus in Sagittarius in the 9th. Retrograde Lucifer in Virgo in the 7th is square the nodal axis.

Retrograde Uranus in Gemini/4th is conjunct the North Node (NN). The SN ruler Jupiter is in Scorpio/9th, sextile Sun-Mars, square retro Pluto in Leo/7th, and inconjunct that Uranus. Uranus is the finger of a yod as well.

The SN in the 10th suggests that in his various lives he is defined by what he does for a living, or who he is in the world/outside the home. Juno conjunct it says that there is a deep level of commitment to that work, but also to maintaining the status quo (10th house). Yet his work is very Uranian, reflecting that he is in fact in touch with his inner Uranus and lets it inform his work. We can know that in some of his lives he has not really learned about and how to "do" Uranus, hence its conjunction to the NN - the SN is where we come from; anything opposite it is opposite where we are. But we know it is part of us, so we can be determined to experience or express that part of ourselves, or feel we do not get to, will not be allowed to, or do not deserve to.

Bowie has integrated his nodes to great effect. He opened the door to his Uranian inner self and has brought it out on stage in many forms over the years. He has explored the effects of actually getting to know and bringing into the public sphere what makes him unique. It is the part of himself that he finds staring back at him when he takes the time to look within. The process has been in making peace with who he is on the inside after not having the freedom to explore it in various lives. It would be easy for Bowie to be successful at something without this inner knowing, yet he would not feel authentic if he did.

Uranus as the finger of a yod puts a tremendous amount of pressure on it. Yods are called "fingers of God" because it can feel that God is pointing at you to do something. The emphasized mission here is to know himself truly and deeply. When young Bowie would have felt an urgency about setting himself apart, even if he was unclear about what in fact *would* set him apart. Trial and error was called for, and I will bet that his early recordings reveal a more conventional composer and singer than we see active in the 1970s when his originality had such a great effect on many other musicians. Uranus is retrograde, so the call to trial and error in self-knowledge is underscored. Others' ways of knowing the self and setting themselves apart just will not work for him.

The SN ruler in Scorpio/9th says that in his various lives he shows up as someone intense who has a strong belief system. The inconjunct to Uranus in the 4th is about receiving extremely difficult feedback he did not know what to do with or how to handle from Uranian sources at home. The criticism Gemini has for

Scorpio is to stop asking hard questions, stop digging below the surface looking for seamy underbellies and hidden truths; just to be here now. Bowie has shown up in different times as serious, intense, interested in taboos including sex, drugs, and rock and roll, and because of this karma will get some serious guff from 4th house folks who live more on the surface of things and prefer all things conventional.

The square of the SN ruler to Pluto in Leo/7th says two things. First, in various lives he is pressured by Leonine others not to behave in Scorpionic ways, or not to believe what he believes. Second it says that his karmic wounding, the deep wounding of the soul that he carries from life to life, involves risking (Jupiter) in the arena of belief (9th).

The karmic wounding at its root is about fairness, equality and justice (7th house). In Leo, he is learning how to express himself. Leo and the 7th says that learning to balance expression within relationship is big on the soul's agenda in his various lives. How much to give, how much to expect to receive, and how to show up in relationship as someone who will accept equality and only equality, are major issues for his learning. His Uranus in the 4th says that inner knowledge and communicating this knowledge are important, yet this Pluto on the Leo Descendant says that he needs someone else, some specific other, to hear him. Pluto is conjunct Moon and Saturn in

Leo/6th, so add to this lots of stuff about family, responsibility, duty, and what he learned from his role models (and what in there needs to be grown beyond) to get a feel for his major growth and healing in this life.

Nicolas Cage

I'm going to focus on a couple of features about his chart to explain why he has always felt different from others and why that feeling has had the important impact on him that it has.

The first thing to note is his South Node in Capricorn in the 1st. By itself this SN placement might seem to speak of someone comfortable with the difficulties life can offer, adept at leadership and standing on his own two feet. Yet with Sun conjunct it, there is a person or influence in his environment who

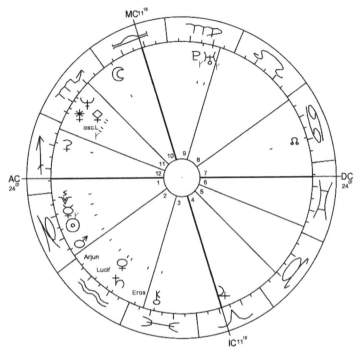

January 7 1964, 5:30 AM, Harbor City CA (rated AA)

is orbited, some powerful and large influence that shines brighter than all the others. Someone else gets a ton of attention for being who he or she is. In this life, that could be seen to be his uncle, Francis Ford Coppola, or the family's acting and creative careers taken all together.

Square the nodal axis is the Midheaven-Nadir axis and Jupiter in Aries conjunct the Nadir. In his various lives, his conditioning (how he is trained to live and be a functioning person) has some sort of confusion about the right balance between work and home, job and family, and outer and inner focus. In most people this results in a need for trial and error about how much emphasis to put on career versus home life, going back and forth to try to find an appropriate balance. This confusion over how to balance inner and outer can lead people to identify with what they do for a living instead of knowing and accepting precisely who they are on the inside when no one else is around.

Jupiter on the IC in this position tells of a risk within the family, or something major happening in the family that interferes with normal family life. Among other things, his mother's experience of mental illness and the effects it had on Cage and his siblings fits with this.

This can manifest like this: He might on a deep level wonder how much faith can he have in himself if his own mother isn't quite right. Part of him might wonder what it means about him that the person who bore him is mentally ill and needs to be institutionalized. Jupiter square the nodes is a statement that he needs to risk believing in himself in order to heal whatever happened in the past that made him doubt the value of true self-knowledge and self-acceptance. His mother is simply one real-world illustration of this energy dynamic he is carrying in his energy field.

The South Node ruler is Saturn in Aquarius in the 2nd house conjunct Venus and square Neptune-Pallas-

Juno-true Black Moon Lilith in Scorpio in the 11th house. His role in his various lives is that he shows up as someone different (Aquarius) and he wants to be a peacemaker and diplomat (conjunct Venus). The square to the energies in the 11th is about friction (square) from groups that challenge his self-worth. The evolutionary intention is to learn from them, but humans have feelings and get hurt when railroaded by Scorpionic sources, especially if one is doing a Venusian "can we all just get along, please?" thing.

Cage comes into this life with karmic imprinting of not being accepted and welcomed by others. He shows up as different and is told as much. His self-esteem has been injured by painful experiences with energies fitting this square. In this life we could pick the press as an example of a source of this energy: a group (11th house) beyond his control (Neptune) that can have harsh (Scorpio) things to say in criticism (square) about his creative work (Saturn-Venus in the 2nd house). Yet it is important to understand that because of this imprinting from his other lives he will *expect* criticism, and even read words about him in a more negative light than they were intended. Until he learns to have faith in himself independent of what others say or seem to imply about him, he will need some trusted confidants in his life to tell him that the criticism is not important.

What Cage is learning karmically is how to develop self-esteem not because of how others see him but because he himself likes who he is. It is one of the regular human journeys, but a bigger deal for him than for most given his karmic conditioning to be hypersensitive to the opinions of others.

The gift of this Chiron should also be noted. Cage has the deep energetic and emotional sensitivity that can help others feel deeply and truly accepted, uniqueness, warts, and all. Cage can learn to bring that energy of compassionate acceptance to others once he has learned to have it for himself – this is the gift of the wounded healer.

Sibel Edmonds

One-time FBI translator and founder of National Security Whistleblowers Association, an independent, nonpartisan alliance focused on government reform and public education.

Edmonds was brought to the FBI as a translator under contract after 9/11, fluent in Turkish, Farsi, and Azerbaijani. A large brouhaha was stirred when, in the course of her work, she accused another translator of covering certain things up. She was blocked; all her efforts to uncover the truth including a court challenge to air all the information were blocked - all in the name of the need for national secrecy. Under a gag order concerning that situation, she continues to work for change through her independent and nonpartisan alliance, the National Security Whistleblowers Coalition.

January 18 1970, 5 AM, Istanbul Turkey (rated A)

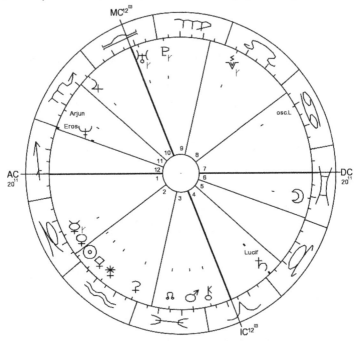

Edmonds' South Node is in Virgo and the 9th house. Square the nodal axis, an unresolved issue, is Moon in Gemini/6th house. As she comes from a background of learning to be clear (Virgo) about what is true or probably true (9th house), there is something new she needs to learn about this Moon. In Gemini/6th, this can come out as needing to learn the right role communication (Gemini) can have in the course of one's duty (6th house), the need to speak up when it is important versus the need to hold one's tongue when it is important, and to be judicious in the use of information while simultaneously ensuring she can sleep at night. This kind of signature arises when one feels an intense need to do something like blow a whistle yet do not because it is not one's job or one's place in the hierarchy to do so. One is just a member of a team and how much does a single voice matter, anyway? Energies in the 6th house learn that fitting in as a cog in a machine is the best use of one's energy – there is no "I" in teamwork, etc. But the conditioning that goes with a Virgo/9th house South Node will instill the importance of following one's conscience and sticking to one's beliefs, so there will be some internal conflict along the way to working out this issue.

The South Node ruler Mercury (her role in her various lives) is retrograde in Capricorn in the 1st house. She shows up in her various lives as competent, mature, sure of herself, and someone with the capacity to lead others yet in need of redefining what leadership and all these things look like and mean (it is retrograde). It is squared by retrograde Uranus in Libra in the 9th house, conjunct the Midheaven. Her soul is trying to learn about Uranian energy (change, individuation and freedom) by receiving friction from powerful Uranian sources: These are sources that drive her to change (square) - change her leadership style, where her energy goes, what she is willing to work for - all Capricorn/1st things. That Uranus is retrograde can mean that the powerful sources are not in line with higher truth and morality (ideal expressions a 9th house Uranus). The retrograde means it is working differently. This is certainly how it has worked in this situation in this life.

The remedy for this kind of karma is to choose work that allows her total freedom of expression and free reign to speak truth and share her beliefs in the public sphere (Uranus in the 9th conjunct the Midheaven). Freelance translation work would fit the bill until she became involved with a government agency during a time in the nation's history when every member of it was so entirely on edge and intolerant of any deviation from the party/nationalistic line (for the record, I have not found mention of work she did prior to that contract with the FBI in 2001). Since the FBI terminated her contract because of her repeated attempts to uncover the truth about the situation, Edmonds has created for herself precisely the kind of role to inhabit that enables her to move beyond her karmic brick walls. She is free to say what she wants, to teach people about what she feels is corruption in the government, and in general to be able to dialogue openly about what her conscience guides her to do, except for the details of the whistle she blew - those are blocked by the government). She has successfully created a role for herself as an agent for change with effects that support her moral compass and brings more truth to light.

That Uranus is retrograde tells us that some trial and error is in order as she has to find her own way to make a place for herself in the world based in her beliefs. Going through that process, while undoubtedly difficult, has enabled her to develop into the kind of leader that karmically is important for her to become.

Her North Node is in Pisces/3rd house. Her karmic growth has a lot to do with aligning with truth (Pisces) and being willing to speak, write about, teach, and disseminate it (3rd house). She has definitely done that in having become unwilling to be silenced. She knows deeply that what she is doing is for the greater good and is pursuing it because of that alignment. There is karmic healing here in learning to be not attached to *particular* truths, but remaining committed to bringing out truths in whatever ways possible. She could have allowed the gag order against speaking freely about her FBI whistle blowing to embitter her and stop her in her tracks, yet she did not. When something like a brick wall comes to you, you can either let it stop you where you are, or you can figure out how to get over or around it in order to keep heading in the direction that is important to you.

Finally, her Pluto is retrograde in Virgo in the 9th. This says that her soul's wounding from past lives is about having chosen the wrong thing to believe in, or refusing to believe in anything at all and realizing that this also does not work. We can imagine her at the end of some other lives on her death bed, reviewing things, gaining clarity on what was really important and regretting (Virgo) the framework into which she fit her life (9th house - belief, philosophy, the search for truth). In some lives, this could be following a religion that she ended up not believing in, or living according to some set of principles that left her feeling bereft of meaning, jaded, or pessimistic. The soul is trying to find the right thing to believe in, to choose an appropriate sort of overarching principle by which to live.

Billie Jean King

Champion tennis player, equal rights activist

November 22 1943, 11:45 AM, Long Beach CA

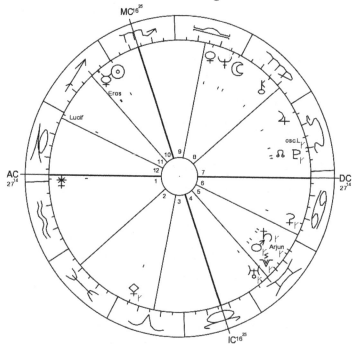

I'm focusing on King's nodal structure, with Pluto in Leo conjunct the 7th house North Node. People born with Pluto in this position often find empowerment through creative expression and recognition for expressing their own personal voices unavailable to them. Expression and recognition could have been blocked by particular individuals or groups or prevented by circumstance.

The South Node in Aquarius says the environments of her various lives are defined by sudden change or trauma, innovation, thinking outside the box, intellectualism and detachment from other parts of life, collective needs and goals, or other modes related to the Uranus/Aquarius archetype. With any of these, it is easy to imagine how personal, creative expression and giving individuals' space to have their voices heard (Pluto in Leo) could be sacrificed to circumstance or the greater good. When communities fall victim to overpowering weather events, for instance, sometimes those who survive must scramble to figure out where food and shelter will be found. In families in which logical thinking and scientific approaches to life are prioritized, a growing young adult in such a family who still wants to paint, dance, and play, and perhaps make a career of it, might not be supported by that family in the way he or she needs. Another example could be in communal environments where the goals of the collective overshadow the goals and needs of the individual, no matter what the individuals feel is in their hearts to express.

Exploring the other side of this, Leonine Plutonian individuals or groups could seem to block the individual, personal expression of individuals, whether or not it is intentional. Imagine a small village that functions well as a community, perhaps as a commune or co-operative type situation, that is so focused on the group that many individuals within the group can identify as part of the whole more than they can as individuals. Imagine that a traveling troupe of players – actors, mimes, dancers, singers – comes through the town every few years. A child living in that town could find herself inspired by seeing these players perform yet have no context or support in the community to pursue expressing her own creativity. Maybe there is no dancing, no singing, no theater in her town when such troupes are not around, so there is no one to teach or support her. Or maybe there is much folk music and dance, but nothing she would consider serious and worthy of taking up, nothing that inspires her. The periodic returns of the troupe become reminders for her that the kinds of self expression that make her feel alive and inspired are out of reach or are not possible for someone like her. The traveling players might come to represent something she never gets to have – this is one way we experience planets and asteroids conjunct our North Nodes. *It's out of reach. It's not what people like us do. It is not what I get to do. Even if I deserved to have, do, or be it, I wouldn't even know where to begin to have, do, or be it.*

With the dual possibilities of feeling they do not deserve it or being determined to have it now because they feel they *do* deserve it, lots of Leonine Pluto opportunities will come to people with this signature. How they respond to them determines whether they turn a new corner karmically or perpetuate the conditioned beliefs that put Pluto conjunct the Leo North Node, making them believe they do not get to be empowered by expressing their creativity.

One thing to note with Pluto conjunct the NN is that in order to empower themselves, people with this signature must separate themselves to one degree or another from the people and places from which they come. The North Node is, relative to the communities into which they're born, somewhere else. Each of our NNs are foreign to our families, and if we are to become empowered (with Pluto on the NN), we will have to go our own ways or find other communities to belong to. Yet as Pluto represents the soul's deepest intentions and desires, this is a major issue these people confront.

King's Pluto-NN in Leo are conjunct the true Black Moon Lilith in the 7th. The karmic need to learn to become empowered have to do with fairness, equality and being heard. The SN is in Aquarius/1st and the ruler Uranus is retrograde in Gemini in the 4th house. The family she was born into is conservative Methodist, representing the Aquarian archetype in not individuating, though we can assume that there were minor quirks in them and the home they made for their children that were notably Aquarian. The ruler retrograde in Gemini in the 4th house says that within such environments, she shows up as someone to whom true self-knowledge is important, but she might not be directly in touch with who she really is (retrogrades tell us the energy is working differently). Opposing Uranus is Mercury in the 10th house, which can manifest as being very aware of conventional ways of living and being confronted by them.

As long as King doesn't truly find out who she really is and therefore cannot tell others, she can find a great deal of success with her people. Telling others who she really is will be a serious challenge for her, one of the hardest things she could undertake. In her mid twenties she realized she was interested in women yet remained married for another seventeen years. She was not able to talk about her sexuality with her parents for almost another decade. Coming out was important for her soul's journey, but having an open dialogue with her conservative, homophobic parents was critical to it. In the 7th, we need to directly connect and communicate with specific others. In this house we have to take risks within our relationships. Doing this with open eyes and an open heart lead King to overcome the feeling of disempowerment and go on to work for equal rights for women in sports and the GLBT community in general, two areas that fit into the 7th house and in which she has had tremendous impact.

Marilyn Manson

Musician

January 5 1969, 8:05 PM, Canton OH (rated AA)

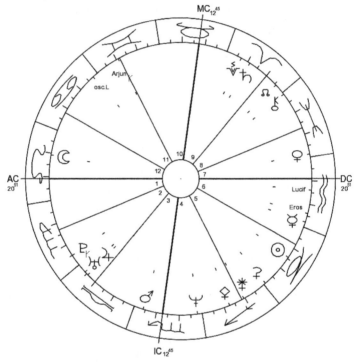

The South Node (SN) in the 2nd says that his soul is coming from environments, his training and conditioning, that have a strong emphasis on values. In Libra, he has been surrounded by politeness, diplomacy, and niceties. The bodies conjunct the SN say that those environments have a lot of the energy of each of these bodies. Jupiter is about belief and faith, Uranus about change and individualism (but just as often conformity and boredom) and Pluto about power.

Ceres-Lilith in opposition is about an argument in those environments between appropriate kinds of emotional expression. Lilith in Cancer needs to let the wildness of emotional realities seek full expression even when they make people uncomfortable. Ceres in Capricorn needs nurturing and care to be practical and conservative. Square the nodes, these parts of life are unresolved issues, meaning that whatever he was taught by his people is not enough for him; he needs to learn to make choices other than those he was taught or makes from habit.

The North Node (NN) in Aries/8th house is about looking unflinchingly into the darker parts of life, developing courage in the face of death and all the parts of life we tend to consider taboo – all the things in his shows and persona that freak many sorts of people out belong to the 8th house. Chiron in Pisces conjunct the NN is a statement that he hasn't been trained to process pain surrounding death and the darker parts of life. Performing and persona-ing as he does is not indicative of whether he has or has not learned to process these things, but in interviews I have seen with him he appears to me to have done so. Chiron in the 8th is a wounding about death, etc., but really about learning to heal our wounding surrounding death. If you are not allowed to mourn a loved one in the way you need, or not permitted to speak of a loved one who has passed away, the unprocessed pain you have about death can result in Chiron in the 8th house conjunct the NN. This Chiron says that in his various lives he is born into families that don't really know how to process the darker parts of life with open eyes and hearts, but he craves doing so.

The SN ruler by sign, Venus, is in Pisces in the 7th. Of the few aspects it makes, the one to work with in order to understand him on deeper levels is the inconjunct between it and Jupiter-Uranus in Libra/2nd. Venus represents his role in his various lives. He will show up as this kind of person and he will be handed roles that fit with this symbolism. The inconjunct tells of his having been knocked off course by religious or believing people with firm values.

The 8th house Aries NN and Chiron in Pisces conjunct it set the stage for why he is intent on doing what appears to most people to be acting out, but this inconjunct adds the juice: *He has been hurt by being knocked off course by elements of conformity and is on a mission to vindicated himself via his creativity.*

He is here to shock people to their cores. It serves as a kind of self-validation that says, *You can't force me to be polite anymore. You can't impinge upon me your morality again. You can't make me shut up or go away. You can't hide the dark truths about life from me or expect me to ignore them.*

Retrograde Pluto is in Virgo in the 2nd house indicates that his deepest karmic, soul wounding is in not getting to live according to his own value system (2nd house), picking what ended up seeming the wrong system (Virgo), and/or getting burned out from trying to make others' value systems work for him (retrograde). At the soul level, his bottom line is in living and creatively expressing himself in any way that feels right to him. He needs to be empowered, but he also needs to make sure the route to empowerment actually leads him to real power. His public comments about wishing he had treated his mother better when he was young illustrate this: He felt empowered by abusing her. Since then he has learned to channel the rebellion and anger he feels into his work.

Looking at his chart with more traditional eyes, we can view his Leo Ascendant and Moon as telling of lots of creative sparks, with Mercury in Aquarius conjunct Eros opposing the Moon adding to them. Mars in Scorpio in the 3rd can be a fiery, dirty, or offensive mouth. We can even see the seriousness with which he takes himself and his work reflected by Saturn-Vesta in the 9th house. Yet to really understand what makes him tick and why he does what he does, we have to add in the karmic angle above.

Oprah Winfrey

Talk Show Host and Media Mogul

January 29 1954, 4:30 AM, Kosciusko MS (rated AA)

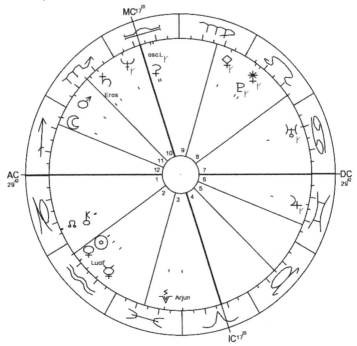

I want to look at two features of her biography from the karmic angle: the near abandonment and sexual abuse in her youth, and her long-term journey with her weight and health.

Winfrey has Uranus conjunct the SN in Cancer in the 7th. This speaks to a karmic history defined by of sudden change and trauma in the family system. The change and trauma leads to unfairness and a lack of balance and justice. This is the environment she was born into, and after abandonment by her teenage mother, her grandmother took her in and initially raised her. Yet she was shuttled later between her mother and other family members, creating a sense of instability fitting with this SN karma.

Her Pluto is in Leo in the 8th house, so she's majoring in learning to be empowered by learning about intense relationships and who in what relationships gets to have what power. It is unfortunately true that some with Pluto in the 8th house manifest abuse of one kind or another, including sexual. Along her soul journey to learn to be empowered in the 8th house, she was abused and raped from the age of nine. At fourteen she gave birth to a boy who died in infancy, death being another 8th house lesson. All 8th house karma is not about sexual abuse, but it does relate to power, sexuality, and who gets what and when. The ideal with this signature is that she would learn to develop very strong boundaries about what she will and will not experience, and to overcome all pain and wounding related to not being able to trust people and reveal herself intimately. Her inborn ability to create a space for people to open up and share their deepest selves is in large part due to what she has learned along her 8th house Pluto journey over many lives: she is empowered by truth and honesty, and by living within that energy, she inspires others to do the same.

Another way of looking at the SN in Cancer is having been conditioned to see the world through an emotional lens. It is not uncommon to see eating disorders and difficult relationships with food in Cancer SNs. Winfrey is wired not just to see the world through an emotional lens, but to feel the world around her. When she gets into habits of unconscious or emotional eating, she gains weight. She knows exactly how to work with those issues in healthy ways and decouple emotions from nutrition, as evidenced by her numerous physical transformations over the years, yet this dynamic is a natural part of her wiring. It is important for her to explore it.

The other side of this is Chiron in Capricorn on the 1st house NN. It represents a need for realistic and radical self-acceptance and self-healing. Karmic growth for her centers in large part on her willingness and ability to put her foot down (Capricorn) with herself (1st house), which will necessitate accepting and loving herself in all the ways that she perceives others cannot and will not love her (Chiron). The dynamic with food and weight is related to this. The idea is that if she tempers the emotionalism she was born with (SN in Cancer) and calms all the triggers of that emotionalism (Uranus in Cancer conjunct the SN), she will inevitably find a host of reasons to feel not good about herself (Chiron in the 1st and in the sign of the judge!).

The cycle of weight gain and weight loss illustrates her ongoing process in learning to balance this nodal structure. Inhabiting this 1st house NN with Chiron on it is about becoming a clear, grounded, realistic person who runs the show of her life with structure, leadership, and discipline. That she has turned that around and offers that leadership to other people is just another level of her growth and becoming an example to others of radical, total and realistic self-responsibility and self-care.

Chapter 9: Celebrities – Life And Death

Since getting deeply into astrology I have been suspect about looking for indicators of the timing of death in people's charts. I felt strongly there must be something else at work, something we cannot see in charts. Just as we cannot see the evolutionary stage of the soul from a person's chart, I believe we cannot see when a particular transit, progression, or solar arc might result in death.

Over the last few years a picture has developed in my mind about new ways to look at health in astrological charts. I begin with energy medicine's perspective that everything is about energy, and then look at a birth chart in terms of energy. Beliefs, attitudes, psychological and emotional knots, physical issues – it is all about energy. Energy is at the root of everything. When we grasp this, how we approach astrology - but really how we approach all of life and our place in the scheme of things - will change.

As a medium I have worked with a number of dead spirits, both those crossed over and those waiting to figure out what happened (that they died) and are not ready to cross. Some have shared with me the greater view on their lives and deaths available only to those who have passed. I have also been guided in meditation back to a death of a previous life associated with my soul, and saw the higher truth of why that life ended when it did even as the man felt he was just getting started with the meaningful part of his life. That life ended abruptly, and it has been important to my journey to accept that it was the right time for that life to end.

> *Why we are born when we do and why we die when we do have everything to do with our soul's journeys and nothing else.*

When it is time to come in, we get ourselves born. When it is time to go out, we die. At the end it is always true that we have accomplished at the soul level what we came here to do. It does not always look like a person is complete when he or she dies (and it does not always *feel* to the person that he or she is done), but from the soul's vantage point, the business is done.

Looking at transit charts for death indicators might seem interesting but we will not find anything concrete that tells us much of anything meaningful. In fact we can look at thousands of charts of dead people and how/when they died and we may see certain patterns seem to emerge, but nothing will be definitive. For example perhaps transiting Mars will seem to indicate accidents or violence in the charts of many deaths. Yet why would a Mars transit for one person result in a cut finger while cutting vegetables, a healthy argument with a spouse for another, yet dying after being hit by a bus or shot in a robbery for another? Why would a Saturn transit mean a long, arduous, and slow death for one person while for another only a challenging new job or the arrival of his or her first child? How is it that a Uranus transit for one person results in breaking free from family constrictions and history while for another some unforeseen and traumatic end?

Accepting the truth that we are born and die when it supports the soul's journey will relieve us of the assumptions and hope that we can predict our death by looking at transits and progressions. Here is what is really going on with this: We hope there is a way to see bad things coming in case we can do something about them. Death inspires a great deal of fear in us on various levels, and we would love to be able to know when it is coming so we can do something to avoid it. The simple truth is that we cannot. When we accept that the journey of the soul is what determines the beginnings and endings of each of our lives, we will be better off and more aligned with the truth about how things work than with fear of what might, can, or will happen to us. Understanding and accepting more truth about life and death will free us to think of and live life differently, which can only improve our quality of life.

Martin Luther King, Jr.

Civil Rights Activist

Born: 15 January 1929, 12:00 PM, Atlanta GA (rated A)

Murdered: 4 April 1968

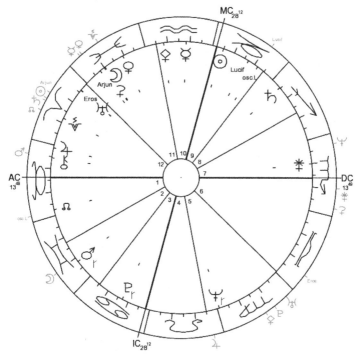

King was majoring in learning the true nature of power (Scorpio SN), learning to establish a solid value system and inhabit it, becoming a leader (both Taurus/1st house NN), and empowering himself through speaking the truth from his heart (Pluto in Cancer/3rd house).

He aligned with and lived what he felt was the truth to the point that when he spoke, he brought that truth to the world around him as an instrument, a channel. King had a profound impact on the social climate and evolution of the United States and inspired many to speak up for what they felt was just.

While his death was tragic we can know for certain that his soul was complete in what it came here to do as Martin Luther King, Jr. How much in his work or personal life might have seemed unfinished from the human vantage point is irrelevant from the perspective of spirit. That he was killed at a young age (39 years old) contributes to the sense of tragedy we have when it comes to his death.

It is perhaps simpler to see the fulfillment of his soul's mission when it comes to King's life than when considering the lives of some other people. When you read the opening paragraph of this section, you had no doubt of its truth. You might have nodded your head upon reading that King came here to become empowered by learning to speak from his heart.

The transits on the day he was shot include Pluto square natal Mars, a transit that might seem to traditional astrological mindsets as indicative of violence. The transit brings challenging opportunities to reorient the expression of will and the desire nature to bring some deep authenticity to a fiery part of ourselves. That is what the energy of the transit is about. No more, no less. In a man who does not speak up for himself this transit could manifest as uncompromising people trying to manipulate him (thereby potentially triggering a strong response that can empower him), or supporting him in finding empowerment by encouraging and teaching him to speak up for himself.

In a woman whose primary way of relating to her sibling is anger, this transit could bring challenges to learn new and varied ways to express Mars energy, perhaps through the entrance into the relationship of a counseling figure or overpowering life or health circumstance that requires her to redirect her energies and be more intentional about her actions and reactions. In a third person, the focus of her life might be steered into new directions by this transit, altering how she understands her desires and how she goes about living them.

That this transit was in play at the time of King's murder is not the reason that he was shot and died. He was killed when he was because what his soul came here to do was complete. He had learned to embody the energy of truth, live according to it, and speak it. That he inspired millions is a side benefit of his personal growth.

Brittany Murphy
Actress and Singer

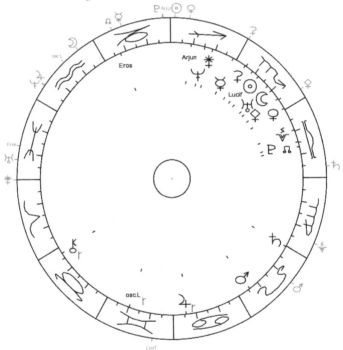

Born: November 10 1977 in Atlanta GA, time unknown.

Murphy was found unconscious on the morning of December 20, 2009 in her home and died soon after.

Murphy's South Node (SN) of the Moon, the repository of emotional memories, lies in Aries. Aspecting the SN is retrograde Jupiter in Cancer in a square to the nodal axis, indicating an unresolved issue. Squares to our nodes are about an energy that trips us up in our various lives, and the way out of that tripping up is to learn to make new choices about and with that energy. With Jupiter, it is about risk. The planet of expansion, belief and faith as a missed step or unresolved issue says that the person has a tendency to risk too much or not enough. It is retrograde, so the energy is now directed inward. Speaking about karma, Jupiter retro square the nodes is the result of some kind of risk-taking behavior that got us in some kind of trouble, and we are probably trying to figure out why. In her soul's other lives, she is trying to figure out how much risk is healthy, how much is enough. How much faith to have in herself, in life, in the world. Retros like this can indicate extreme overdoing in other lives (needing now to direct the energy inward to regroup or recharge), or extreme underdoing in other lives (needing now to direct the energy inward for the same reasons) or perhaps both, trying to figure out the right middle path by risking the extremes.

In the sign of Cancer, this is about risk, belief and faith through the lens of emotion. This sign is all about feeling, feeling into things, reading the emotional energy of a room, nurturing – learning how to open the heart and experience life by feeling. Retro Jupiter in Cancer squaring the nodes is about taking risks of the heart, and attempting to recover from risks that did not go so well. The learning here is not to open or close the heart, but to learn to make new choices about matters of the heart, when it is a good idea to risk it and when it is maybe not.

This explains Murphy's heart murmur. With traditional medical astrology we might look to the Sun/Leo/5th house archetype specifically about the heart, perhaps to Mars/Aries/1st house for the bodily issues, and then more generally to Mercury/Virgo/6th for indications of illness and disease. Looking at the chart in terms of energy and karma shows that she carried confusion and probably wounding about having risked too much or not enough in affairs of the heart.

Another contribution of energy medicine is that the physical body will conform to the energy held in our other bodies (emotional, etheric, mental, etc.).[13] With pain from having risked too much (*I poured out my heart to my one true love and was rejected*) or not enough emotional expression (*I never told my one*

---

[13] This is the basis of medical intuition, by the way. Check out the work of Louise Hay and Caroline Myss for educational and highly relevant explorations and tales of medical intuition.

true love of my feelings and feel heart sick from it)
still carried in her emotional body as she was born in
this life, Murphy manifested a heart murmur. Her
physical body's heart conformed to the energetic kink
in her emotional body, the emotional part of her that
is carried from life to life.

What is imbalanced energetically that we don't
know how to deal with will manifest as physical issues
in time, without fail. "Deal with" means to process, to
understand and most importantly let go. It means to
not cling to the pain of what we experience and the
meaning we affix to why it happened to us and to
grieve what needs to be grieved and then move on.
We are of course changed by the situation, the feelings
and the overall experience, but we don't have to hold
energy in our various bodies, just waiting to manifest
physically. I see situations like this all the time in my
work and in fact help people with persistent physical
issues to get to the root of what is happening to
alleviate the need for physical manifestations to
continue. The clients who ask me for this are intrepid
to say the least, as this is a fast lane on the highway of
spiritual growth.

Said simply, Murphy brought into this life pain
from risk in emotional arenas in other lives. The
intention of her soul is to learn about emotion via
risking big expressions of emotion, yet the experiences
a person has along that kind of journey can leave deep

impacts on the emotional body. The result of still carrying that emotional pain unprocessed at birth was the heart murmur that may turn out to be the cause of her death. As of this writing, the toxicology report has not yet been released from the Coroner's Office.

I know that I see that Jupiter-in-Cancer in her acting work. There were moments in her films when I was shocked by the directness and power of her expression - Jupiter in Cancer is, on a practical level, "big emotion/big heart."

Why did Brittany Murphy die the way she did when she did? Because her soul was complete with what she came here to do. Her learning for this chapter was complete. It was time for her soul to move on.

Chapter 10: Suicide

It feels right to end a book about the journey of the soul through many lifetimes with some discussion of death. Earlier in the book you read about the input the soul takes from its experiences in many lives and what happens between lives, and Chapter 9 includes some frank discussion about death. Suicide isn't the norm and when it affects us, it does so very deeply. This chapter is offered in the spirit of inspiring honest dialogue that might lead to healing.

Suicide is a difficult topic for many of us. It can seem incomprehensible why someone would do it. We can look at chronic depressive or disease states and in certain cases understand the choice, but even that sometimes doesn't help. Again, the fact is that a person is born when he or she is to suit the journey of the soul. A person dies when he or she does for the same reasons. Suicide, because it is a choice, might seem to not fit with the soul's journey, but it does.

Just as with any other death, the soul withdraws from the physical body at the moment of death. There is an opportunity to go to the light if the individual is open to it. As most suicides have lost hope of finding meaning or creating health and happiness, most are not immediately greeted by loved ones welcoming them to their next phase (remember that this is entirely dependent upon the person's openness to it). As with all deaths, the process of getting to the next phase, what is required, and how long that lasts is unique to each individual, depending upon on how open he or she is to accepting the lessons of his or her life from the bird's eye view.

What Suicide Means For The Soul's Journey
Forget religious teachings you have heard about the impact of suicide. There is no place called hell that is the automatic destination for someone who ends his or her own life. There is no regression back to "lower" life forms (amoebas, rocks, or trees) waiting for such a person. There is nothing external that is bad waiting for such a person.

The impact on the soul's journey is that the violence perpetrated on the self must be dealt with in other lives. The soul will register the disempowerment, unhappiness, and/or poor health leading up to the decision as kinds of manifestations of particular beliefs and behaviors. The soul will understand that the routes leading to violence to one's self didn't work, and that other routes fitting with the

250

chosen life themes must be explored. Suicide is an expression of free will and the soul does not judge. The experience is taken as one of many possible experiences, one choice among many, and the feelings and experiences noted as part of the education of what it means and takes to live human lives on Earth.

The emotional process leading up to the suicide, as well as the violence of it, do carry over into other lives. Whether it shows up as a general sense of having been traumatized or being self-destructive will depend on a few factors, primarily the reasons assigned for the suicide. *Is everything my fault? Someone else's? God's? My body's (in the case of illness)?* Whatever the attitude at death, it is imprinted on the non-physical bodies and a person is born into other lives with the imprint. A woman angry at God who kills herself from a place of anger will come into other lives with that same anger. A man who kills himself because he perceives himself as a failure will come into other lives with the same attitude. A person who suicides in one life won't in each life kill him or herself, but the powerlessness, anger, guilt, shame, or hopelessness that inspired the ending of another life will be present in the emotional baseline of that soul's other lives.

Some of my clients living with extreme powerlessness, anger, guilt, shame, and/or hopelessness sometimes admit to having suicidal thoughts. The vast majority of them are clear that suicide is not something they will do, yet they know their persistent suicidal thoughts or references mean something important. To the vast majority of us, it doesn't feel normal to have such a voice inside us.

It can happen that people with such thoughts have committed suicide in other lives. Most will have a gut feeling if it is something they have done or may have done at one time or another. My strategy for working with them begins with helping them fully accept the possibility that are capable of treating themselves with that kind of violence. There are such intense judgments about suicide that along with any memories or thoughts related to it, the judgments go along, too. Accepting one's actions and forgiving the self is necessary. It is an important step in healing the memory of having done violence to one's self. I also help them understand that they now have tools, resources, and skills they probably didn't have in another life in which suicide seemed the best option. As stated, the vast majority of them know this is not where they are headed and are willing to learn to love themselves more this time around.

The Astrology of Suicide

Astrologically, there are many different ways that a suicide in a past life can show up in the birth chart. More often than not, what will show up is an indicator of the pressures felt that lead to the decision.

Also showing up will be indicators of difficulty in learning to love the self no matter what is happening in a person's life. This is another way of describing disempowerment, and it can show up in various ways. What is important in this discussion is to understand the mental and emotional states that can lead to self-destructive behavior, more than any specifics about suicide or the fear that someone will do it.

This is key:

There is no specific set of symbols that will tell us if a person has committed suicide in a past life, and we cannot see in a chart if a person will choose to end his or her life.

Our experience of any archetype can lead to shame, guilt, anger, powerlessness, depression, and hopelessness. In the Moon/Cancer/4th house archetype, being disowned by family or losing a home could do it. In Saturn/Capricorn/10th house, losing a job or elected office that provides a certain level of income and status could do it if enough meaning and self-esteem are attached to that status. With Mars/Aries/1st house, we could feel our wills annihilated by any number of possible human experiences. In the Pluto/Scorpio/8th house archetype, we can become so depleted from trying to learn about power through abusive relationships that we end up despondent.

Some astrological indicators that could tell of suicide in another life include:

But wait, here is the important part again:

There is no specific set of symbols that will tell us if a person has committed suicide in a past life, and we cannot see in a chart if a person will choose to end his or her life.

What the symbols tell us is about the energetic dynamics in a person's imprint, which is the way it is because of that person's karma. This list only scratches the surface of possible configurations. I offer this information to help you gain understanding and develop context when working with someone who has such destructive thoughts. When you see any of these configurations, do not assume that a person did commit suicide in another life or will do so in this one.

Pluto conjunct the NN: Karmically conditioned to believe one doesn't get to develop personal power.

Saturn conjunct the SN: Lives defined by hardship can instill a belief that one will never getting a leg up, and that peaceful living and easy health are impossible.

Mars square the nodes: Misuse of will, perhaps in anger or violence, and perhaps toward self.

Venus square the SN ruler: Beliefs that relationships never work, there is no support when one needs help, one cannot trust anyone.

SN in the 8th house: Beliefs that everyone else gets to have power, everybody else's demands matter more than one's own.

SN in the 6th house: Beliefs that life is drudgery and equality is impossible, one will always be second class.

SN in the 12th house: Beliefs that life is a prison, there is no meaning to be had, life and/or God can screw you whenever it/he wants.

These are extremes. If you have any of these listed, you might sense that a part of you resonates with the energy of the statement but not strongly enough to do yourself harm. To some degree powerlessness, hopelessness, anger, and pain are a natural part of the human experience. They are part of what we find as we go about learning what it means to live in bodies like these, in places and times like these.

Client Chart 12

Born: September 3 1972, 12:55 PM, Downey CA

Committed suicide: May 17 2009

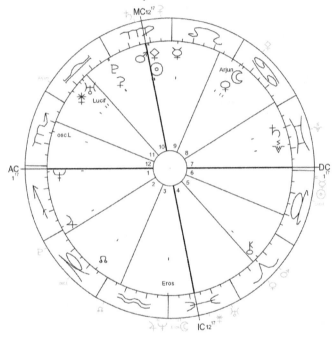

This woman came in for a session to talk about her long-term depression and deep sense of physical and emotional fatigue. She had sought many forms of healing support and help, and nothing had worked. She knew about the combination of modalities I use (evolutionary astrology, mediumship, relaying messages from spirit guides, and some shamanic soul-retrieval techniques), having been referred by a friend of hers who had been a client in previous months and for whom I had done some soul retrieval and to whom I had taught some useful meditative techniques.

From within a meditative state, I was shown that she had energetic ties to an individual with less than healthy intentions. He was a subject of her academic graduate work, and she was told by others that he practiced "black magic." Her guides instructed me that the best course of action was to teach her meditative techniques to develop and maintain healthy energetic boundaries. It was absolutely in her power to take her energy back, yet she didn't believe that she could do so. The majority of the session was spent supporting her in locating and getting to know the parts of her that were powerful and could say "no" to people and to energies.

Her South Node is in Cancer in the 8th house, indicating that she is conditioned karmically to be aware of the needs of people around her, and also the power dynamics present in every relationship and part of life. This combination can result in an extreme feeling that one does not have any power to speak of. It is also a signature of being skilled in manipulating others, but this isn't how it manifested in her life.

Neptune is conjunct the Sagittarius Ascendant, which brings the porousness of Neptune to her body and sense of self. People with Neptune in this placement can feel there is no such thing as boundaries, and if there were, there might be no way to develop them.

Her North Node is in Capricorn in the 2nd house. This means that learning to be realistic about her worth and value as a human being was paramount to her karmic growth. Chiron in Aries in the 5th is square the nodal axis, representing unresolved issues in dealing with pain and suffering, and the wound in Aries is specifically to the sense of getting to stand up for herself and say "no" when it was needed to maintain her health and sanity. It will have begun in her infancy, imprinting her that her sense of having the right to have boundaries was diminished.

Lucifer and Juno in Libra/11th are also square the nodes. Lucifer manifests as a voice of doubt within us. Juno represents commitment, and these two in Libra square the nodes echoes the Chiron configuration in its doubt that she gets to have boundaries. From what I knew of her life, she had healthy relationships with her sister and other family members, and was happily married. Energetic boundaries seemed the primary issue at hand.

The transits at the time of her death include Saturn conjuncting her Sun-Mars-Midheaven, Mars conjunct her Chiron, and Pluto square her natal Pluto-Ceres. Saturn coming to Mars-Sun-MC challenge one to introduce more structure to one's self-expression, assertion, and place in the world. This woman had been increasingly absorbed in her personal health situation for months. Mars conjunct Chiron can trigger some kind of overt situation to bring one's wounding to light. Yet she was conscious of her lack of boundaries at least at the time of the session she had with me.

The Pluto square can bring up our deepest fears, with the goal of learning to overcome them. At this time we are invited to learn to live in spite of our fears and to learn to come into our own power. Her natal Pluto is conjunct Ceres in Libra. This says to me that this soul's wounding and fears have to do with becoming empowered through loving herself, and to experience this with other people. With this configuration it can be that we wait for someone else to come along (Libra) in order for our healing to occur. It can also come out as being confident in enlisting help when one needs it. In this woman, it manifested as beliefs about how empowered she could be in her relationships, and with regards to caring for her own health.

She had the power to develop healthy boundaries, as each of us does. Yet she didn't believe it. It is not the Pluto transit that explains her choice to end her life. It is that she didn't believe she could be empowered enough to take care herself, and this is an issue in her soul's many lives.

A student of mine at the time was friendly with the woman. When she learned of the suicide, she called me. During our conversation, a handful of days after the event, the spirit of the woman came to me. As I spoke with her friend, I was aware of the deceased woman taking in what I was telling my student about my impressions from having worked with her. She was in the process of wrapping up her life by going to those who survived her and cared for her, observing them in their grief, learning about herself objectively from their grieving processes. It seemed to me that seeing herself through my eyes, and via my conversation with my student, helped her put that feeling of powerlessness into a perspective she didn't have when alive. Grasping the entire picture of her life and how it fit with her soul's journey would require her to go into the light, which she had at that time not been ready to do. When the conversation ended and she was leaving, I was left with the impression that for the first time, she understood the role of her choice in life and, now dead, crossing over was entirely up to her when she was ready to do so.

David Foster Wallace

Novelist, Essayist and Short Story Writer

Born: February 21 1962, Ithaca NY, time unknown

Committed suicide: September 12 2008

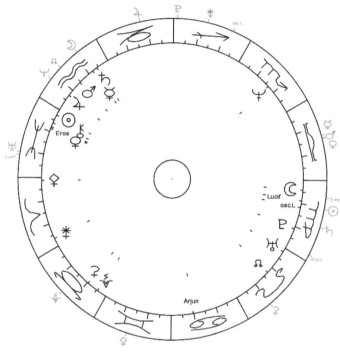

Wallace is best known for his sprawling novel *Infinite Jest*, a non-linear exploration of the human pursuit of pleasure and what can happen when we get it. He was subject to depression, and had been on an anti-depressant for a number of years before experiencing severe side effects. He ceased taking that one and pursued other treatments, with nothing working. When he resumed taking the original medication, he found that it had lost its efficacy. He hung himself in his basement on September 12, 2008.

We don't have a birth time for Wallace, but a lot of important information can be seen without it. His nodal structure includes retrograde Neptune in Scorpio squaring the Aquarius South Node. This is the mark of a search for meaning. In his soul's various lives, he is looking for the right ways to connect to alternate modes of reality, exploring means of connecting with the divine or non-local identification of self. What we need from such connection is a sense of meaning, and with Neptune square the nodes, meaning is not always found. Wallace had been through a narcotics addiction and recovery in his early thirties, and recreational drugs are one manner people alter their states of consciousness. It is just one example of a Neptunian choice that didn't work for him.

An image I get associated with this nodal structure is of someone in a village in a traditional culture. The medicine people in the village use chemical substances to alter their consciousness to do their shamanic work. There is a boy in the village who sees their work and knows about the substances they use to achieve it. He wants to do that work, healing work, yet maybe he isn't chosen by the shamans to follow that path. He is neither born into a family of healers nor called by the gods to do that work, the two ways shamans are identified and chosen in traditional cultures. His disappointment could make him feel that he doesn't get to have the meaningful life he sees others getting to live. He might attach meaning, a belief, to the use of substances as a route to finding meaning in life, and have other lives using substances in attempts to achieve that meaning. This is just one kind of story to go with this Neptune square the nodal axis, but it illustrates the dynamics of the karma associated with it.

His retrograde Pluto is in Virgo, opposing Sun-Chiron-Eros in Pisces. The soul's intention is to get specific in order to improve something, to do something really well. That it is retrograde says that to be empowered through the lens of Virgo, he has to let go of external notions of power and ways to get there to figure out his own ways to empowerment. The karmic wounding involves confrontation with woundedness in the realm of spiritual things (opposing Chiron in Pisces), adding to the pressure of needing to find meaning in life indicated by the square of Neptune to the nodes. Reading the Sun as the chairman of his internal board meeting, he had to experience first-hand a Piscean sensitivity as he tried to learn to heal the missteps of Neptune's square to the nodes and Pluto's opposition to Chiron-Sun in Pisces.

The bottom line of all of this is that his relationship with substances as a route to meaning had been played out when he entered recovery in the early 1990s. When the prescribed medication he had taken for depression was proven to have lost its effectiveness, he made the choice to end his life, giving in to the depression he had lived with for decades.

The transits at the time of his death include retrograde Neptune conjunct natal Jupiter, retrograde Chiron conjunct natal Mars, and Saturn had recently finished a pass over his Pluto, highlighting the opposition to the bodies in Pisces.

Neptune transits to Jupiter can erode our faith. The evolutionary intention is to learn to release all in our belief systems that is not useful, meaningful, and connects us to ultimate truth. Neptune calls for everything non-essential to dissolve, so we can be left with truth, which is almost always simpler than how we usually build our worldviews. It can leave us feeling depleted regarding meaning and the search for it, yet we then choose to go with whatever is left. This is how we can build a scaffold of meaningfulness to move ahead with our lives.

Chiron transiting Mars can bring energetic and emotional sensitivity to his experience of expression of will and desire. Chiron times are necessarily inner, quiet times. The effect can be to dampen one's sense of expression of will, no matter how much get-up-and-go a person might naturally have. Ideally, Martian impulses inside us are redirected to include deeper levels of energetic and emotional sensitivity so that we can use our will in the direction of living with more compassion. With Chiron conjunct his Sun natally, he was already full of this energetic and emotional sensitivity, and with the natal opposition to Pluto, he wasn't always comfortable dealing with the portion he already possessed.

Saturn transiting in conjunction to Pluto can bring a heaviness regarding how we are doing with our life missions, and can be a depressive influence and bring up all sorts of elements of our deepest karmic wounding. Typical astrological thinking would be inclined to ascribe such a Saturn transit as the reason for deepening depression or suicide, but such a transit would never be the entire story of any suicide.

Yet none of these transits are why he took his own life. They no doubt contributed to his mood, but he killed himself because he no longer believed that his depression could be helped, and that he could not stand living with it any longer if it couldn't be helped. He hung himself because he chose to do so.

About The Author

Tom Jacobs is an evolutionary astrologer, medium, and channel with an active private practice with clients around the country and around the globe. A member of evolutionary astrologer Steven Forrest's Apprenticeship Program since 2004, his work supports people to uncover and connect deeply with what their souls are here to do.

His original work on the Lilith archetype and emotional healing are reflected in the two original natal reports available via his website, "The True Black Moon Lilith Natal Report" and "Living in the Present Tense: A Personalized Astrological 2012 Prep Course". He teaches karmic astrology and intuitive skills development both privately and to groups. Tom has a special interest in how health is affected by karma, including how karma shows up in astrological birth charts and how we can improve our health by healing karma.

Tom holds a bachelor's degree in philosophy from The College of Wooster (Wooster, OH). He is the author of several books and his writings on astrology and spirituality have appeared in Dell Horoscope Magazine, Aspects Magazine, and InnerChange Magazine.

Contact Tom via his website, www.tdjacobs.com.

Made in the USA
Monee, IL
26 April 2022